BEFORE I CLOSE MY EYES

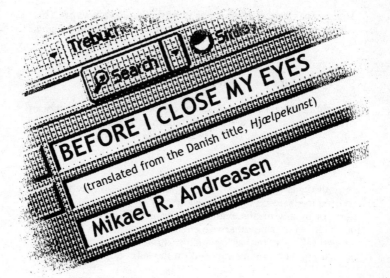

BEFORE I CLOSE MY EYES

(translated from the Danish title, Hjælpekunst)

Mikael R. Andreasen

HODDER

Copyright © 2006 by Mikael R. Andreasen
(mikael@washington-inc.net)
English translation copyright © 2006 Ben Sand
Cover photograph copyright © 2006 Christian Mailand

The original Danish edition was published as *Hjælpekunst*. This
edition is published by arrangement with Claudia Böhme Rights
and Literary Agency, Hannover, Germany
(www.agency-boehme.com)

First published in Great Britain in 2006

1

British Library Cataloguing in Publication Data
A record for this book is available from the British Library

ISBN 0 340 90900 5

Printed and bound in Great Britain by
Bookmarque Ltd, Croydon, Surrey

The paper and board used in this paperback are natural
recyclable products made from wood grown in sustainable
forests. The manufacturing processes conform to the
environmental regulations of the country of origin.

Hodder & Stoughton
A Division of Hodder Headline Ltd
338 Euston Road
London NW1 3BH

www.madaboutbooks.com
www.hodderbibles.co.uk

CONTENTS

If one is truly to succeed in leading a person
to a specific place,
one must first and foremost take care to find him
where he is
and begin there.
This is the secret in the entire art
of helping.
Anyone who cannot do this
is himself under a delusion
if he thinks he is able to help
someone else.
In order truly to help someone else,
I must understand
more than he but certainly first and foremost understand
what he understands.
If I do not do that,
then my greater understanding
does not help him
at all.

Søren Kierkegaard (Danish philosopher)

INTRODUCTION

Together with my good friend, Christian, I run a part-time company in Copenhagen, Denmark, which we call Washington Inc. We occupy ourselves with pictures and sounds, organise some photo work and give out a couple of CDs now and then. We also import CDs and vinyl, which we sell in our small store in the apartment I live in. The shop draws a varied crowd, from close friends to friends of friends, all there to help themselves to some new music. Complete strangers have also been known to pop in – Stine was one of these strangers.

Through an internet music forum she found out about our small distribution label, and one spring day in 2002 the doorbell rang. She ended up listening to a couple of records, buying a few, and then leaving. It didn't take long before she returned.

In the following months she became an increasingly frequent visitor, and it often ended up in long conversations about music. Since Stine and I, in many respects, share a similar taste in music, we naturally began going to concerts together. As the months passed, our conversations remained tangled in music, genres, small obscure record companies and the obligatory rants about the weather. Neither of us touched on deeper, personal issues, therefore I hadn't felt the need to tell her that I was a Christian. At least not until, after sending a few chatty emails back and forth, Stine, presumably in jest, brought to a close that evening's email with the following sentence: '. . . if you could explain to me the meaning of life before I close my eyes tonight, I would be content . . .'

That sentence invoked long and intense email exchanges about God, faith and doubt. The following book contains, in simplified form, the dialogue that was created via the emails between us in the subsequent months.

It is my hope that this book will offer some insight to those picking it up.

Mikael R. Andreasen

- - -

From: Stine Forsberg
Sent: November 19, 2002 10:44 pm
To: Mikael R. Andreasen
Subject: Re:

. . . if you could explain to me the meaning of life before I close my eyes tonight, I would be content . . .

- - -

From: Mikael R. Andreasen
Sent: November 19, 2002 10:56 pm
To: Stine Forsberg
Subject: Re:

The meaning of life? Hmm, to become friends with God would be my best answer, but perhaps that's too abstract?

From: Stine Forsberg
Sent: November 19, 2002 10:58 pm
To: Mikael R. Andreasen
Subject: Re:

Do you believe in God?

From: Mikael R. Andreasen
Sent: November 19, 2002 11:03 pm
To: Stine Forsberg
Subject: Re:

Absolutely. Although, even if I didn't, I think that would probably be the best answer I could come up with. ☺

From: Stine Forsberg
Sent: November 19, 2002 11:09 pm
To: Mikael R. Andreasen
Subject: Re:

I'm going to have to think about that, but it's going to have to be while I'm asleep. Seriously, though, if you suggest that there's meaning to life, then I assume you've already found it? I think it's quite difficult to get my head around those things . . .

Sleep well, Mikael!

– – –

From: Mikael R. Andreasen
Sent: November 19, 2002 11:15 pm
To: Stine Forsberg
Subject: Re:

Think it over. ☺

I would be curious to hear what you'd come up with. Feel free to ask me questions if there's anything you're wondering about. I am happy to talk about my faith, especially to be challenged and provoked myself.

But yeah, sleep well. I too should be heading to bed. I don't feel too well, perhaps a little fever, or just a lack of sleep!

Anyway, goodnight and sleep well!

All the best from here,

Mikael

– – –

From: Stine Forsberg
Sent: November 20, 2002 9:08 pm
To: Mikael R. Andreasen
Subject: Re:

After a long and pleasant day at a teacher colleague's party at David's house, with lots of blackberry pie and tea, I am finally at home. I can't wait for this day to end . . . I am so tired. Thank you for yesterday.

I found it impossible to sleep last night and lay in bed thinking and thinking. At one point I was ready to jump on my bike and ride over to you, but didn't. What would have been the point?

It feels strange to say this – especially on email – but I have wanted to talk to you about this for some time now, I just didn't dare. That probably sounds dumb, but it's true.

I don't personally believe in God, but would like to find out exactly why it is that I don't. Besides, with my adherence to science there leaves no room for a personal God – if you understand what I mean. I am, however, rather intrigued by the 'big' existential questions – why I, for instance, have become caught up with you. ☺ It irritates me that I have taken (and still take) the important things in this world for granted . . . and I really don't know anyone who actually believes in God. Trust me, it's a new experience. None of this probably makes any sense, but it's what I was thinking while cycling home. I don't want to inflict my problems on you so they become a burden, but it is nice to be able to write to someone.

I hope you didn't get sick yesterday, you did mention that you weren't feeling too well.

Stine

- - -

From: Mikael R. Andreasen
Sent: November 20, 2002 11:45 pm
To: Stine Forsberg
Subject: Re:

Hi Stine,

Thank you so much for your email. It was exciting to read. Thank you for daring to be honest. Hmm . . . how can I respond to that? I would really like to be at your disposal – if I can – and come up with some comments on your existential conclusions. If so, then it's only fair that you know where you find me and what it is I believe. As I mentioned before, I believe in God. To me, fellowship with him is to see the alpha and omega in daily life, although I don't always contribute as much as I should to that relationship. Why is that, Mikael? And how? Good questions. I generally take a scientific approach to many things in life; I am normally a sceptical and down-to-earth person. On the other hand, it's difficult to deny God when you have experienced that he is real. When he responds to questions you ask him. When he offers us comfort, encouragement. When he . . .

I am only touching on this very briefly, but I would love to elaborate on it in a proper conversation. I just want you to know that under no circumstances should you feel that I am trying to manipulate or convert you to believe in what I am saying. Obviously I believe in God and that he wants a personal relationship with everyone, and that personal relationship is the highest thing I could wish for anyone else. However, the path to God has to be through each individual's own decisions and wishes. It's not the potential end-product of me sitting here and writing a thousand words which end up with you having an epiphany.

Did it come as a shock to you that I believe in God? I would admit to being slightly surprised if that were the case. There are more than a few hints on our Kloster record.[1] Jan-Erik, and all of my friends from Glorybox believe in God, not to mention the guys from This Beautiful Mess, Damien Jurado, Rosie Thomas, Pedro the Lion, Loch Ness Mouse, etc., etc., etc.[2] The common thread that all these artists share is that they allow their beliefs to influence their music, but not in the way many other Christian artists do, which is to use their music as a means to preach to people. Since their beliefs are such a natural part of their lives, it would almost be strange if there were no traces of this in their music. I think it could revolutionise your thoughts and preconceptions of what belief is, and what Christians are, if we began to discuss this further. Hopefully I would be able to show you that Christianity is not about rules and regulations or about restrictions or straightjackets for people's expression. In reality, it's a source of freedom and creativity. Again, for me these things are so important but I don't want them to come across as 'preachy'. I want to share what I believe, and would very much like to hear your own reflections and thoughts on the greater meanings of life. If you want, you are more than welcome to drop by tomorrow evening around 7.30. I will be away tomorrow from 7.30 am till 7.30 pm, and the room is quite a mess (since I was ill), but who cares? It would be great if you could reply this evening if you intend to come over (if you haven't already gone to bed). If it's not convenient or you don't feel like it, that's fine.

That's all for this time.

Adios,

Mikael

– – –

From: Stine Forsberg
Sent: November 21, 2002 7:26 am
To: Mikael R. Andreasen
Subject: Re:

Hi Mikael,

Thanks so much for your reply.

You just caught me on my way to work, so I'll have to write more this afternoon. Thanks for the invitation to come over tonight. I would have loved to, but have been invited to a friend's house for dinner.

Changing subjects, the way you explained your beliefs to me didn't come across as preachy. Your faith shines through on many points. The reason I asked you in the first place was that I was interested in talking about it, but didn't dare to ask you. It's strange to know something so meaningful about another person, but not because someone else has told you. Believe me, I have cycled home from your house more than once feeling confused and spinning. It's difficult to write anything rational, I think.

Anyway, I have to cycle to work now. Hope you're feeling better, have a great day!

Stine

- - -

From: Stine Forsberg
Sent: November 21, 2002 7.18 pm
To: Mikael R. Andreasen
Subject: Re:

Hi Mikael,

I'm finally home.

I got your last email after I had already gone to bed, which is why I didn't reply. I hope you managed to read my email this morning before you left for work.

Now, to the point: I'm slightly afraid of what I'm about to say. I don't want to hurt or offend you in any way, but it could come to that. Naturally I don't know your boundaries, but if only you knew how many prejudices I have had and how many others are still lurking in some dark corner of my mind. I would really like to broaden my horizons, but have lived so much of my life without that desire. It has only been in the past few weeks that I have begun contemplating these things, or felt a need to do so. You have no idea how many quiet moments I have spent alone lately just thinking and thinking and thinking. It feels great to finally set words to thoughts. I can't help but remark on how the email you sent yesterday sounded so beautiful and well thought out. I have always considered myself superior to Christians, but recently it's been the complete opposite. In fact, I have almost felt inferior, possibly because I am envious that you/they are convinced about something that most people in my circle of friends have no opinion on. I have always taken existence for granted and not bothered to occupy myself with how it all came about.

The possibility that someone has been alive for eternity is a topic I never thought important enough to warrant attention. Although I am almost convinced that I will never believe in God, if he does exist then I would like to find out. That seems a tall order, though, for someone who doesn't believe. In the end, perhaps I don't even want to know (probably due to my own prejudices). Even though the reasons and excuses for not wanting to find out are some of the dumbest you could find, I want to understand why it is I don't believe in God, for my own sake. I will round it all off with the world's worst compliment. Previously, without a doubt, I would have ended any form of such contact because I don't really understand Christianity – in part due to prejudices that don't complement my way of thinking. Laugh it off or take it to heart, I'm not bothered, but it's true. You have changed that.

Anyway, have a good evening – I hope you had a good day.

Stine

– – –

From: Mikael R. Andreasen
Sent: November 21, 2002 9:17 pm
To: Stine Forsberg
Subject: Re:

Hi Stine,

Thanks for your email.

First and foremost, at no point in time were you in danger of overstepping my boundaries. ☺ In other words, you can write exactly what it is you think about belief, Christians or Christianity and I will not get offended. I know it's a big promise to make, but I am confident I can keep it. This is partly down to the fact that it takes a lot to offend me, but more due to the fact that I myself have been down long trails of thought as to the circumstances surrounding a life without God. I do not find it hard to relate to the prejudices people can have – many of them have elements of truth in them. In the end it's just as much the Christian's fault as anyone else's.

Before I go on, I want to come back to something you wrote in your email yesterday: 'Changing subjects, the way you explained your beliefs to me didn't come across as "preachy". Your faith shines through on many points. The reason I asked you in the first place was that I was interested in talking about it, but didn't dare to ask you. It's strange to know something so meaningful about another person, but not because someone else has told you. Believe me, I have cycled home from your house more than once feeling confused and spinning.'

I can't resist being curious and asking which points it was where you felt my faith shone through – and would be grateful if you care to elaborate on what it is that has made you feel confused and left your head spinning. It would be interesting for me to find out what kind of signals I am sending out, and how they are being interpreted by a person relatively unknown to me. I completely respect your stance on not being able to believe in God, but would love to change your picture of Christianity just a bit. I have two books that I would like to lend you. Both of them take up varying aspects of Christianity, yet are not written in a dogmatic or evangelistic way. There are very few Christian books that I myself enjoy reading, but these two are fantastic. I have lent them to other friends of mine who were very critical in relation to faith (not that they became Christians after reading the books), but their understanding of the subject was changed just a little.

The first book is by C. S. Lewis and is simply called *Mere Christianity*. He also wrote the *Chronicles of Narnia*, which I assume you've heard of? The *New York Times* wrote the following about him: 'C. S. Lewis, also known as the skeptic's apostle, is the ideal writer for the doubting, those who stand on the halfway line and would like to be Christian, yet are hindered by their intellect.' The other book is called *The Jesus I Never Knew*, written by a journalist called Philip Yancey. All I can say is it's fantastic. The book is written in such a way that you never feel as though he is forcing you to think or believe something you yourself don't want to. If you'd like to borrow them, I'd be happy to lend them to you – if not, that's fine too. The books are not meant as an alternative to our own talks, but more as a supplement. It would also be great to meet up soon, either here or in the north-west. I also have a video I would like to show you. Jan-Erik, Solrun, Sarah and Jan from Glorybox and I go to the same church. A few weeks ago we led the worship at a meeting. I didn't realise it was being recorded, but it was, and the sound is actually quite good. There are so many things I would love to talk to you about, but I think it's better if you dictate where the conversations go. I can completely understand the point you made earlier about feeling superior to Christians. In fact, I consider such a feeling natural. However, when you mention your recent feeling of things turning around, I only hope that through communicating with me you'll never feel inferiority, but instead find peace in your own conclusions.

At no point in time do I want you to feel it's a sign of weakness or inferiority that you have all these unanswered questions and walk around a bit confused about things. Haven't we all been there?

Stine, I've been a motor-mouth. It's been a long day; all I want to do is sit down and watch a video before I go to bed.

Anyway, I've had a great day, albeit long. I hope yours has been as good.

All the best,

Mikael

- - -

From: Stine Forsberg
Sent: November 21, 2002 10:59 pm
To: Mikael R. Andreasen
Subject: Re:

Hi Mikael,

When I sit and think about it and try to find examples, I guess music is the best place to start. As you said before, that's where faith shines through very obviously. When I first heard the Kloster record it came as quite a shock. It was very honest and direct.

Another thing that made it shocking was that I received it very shortly after meeting you. It's no secret that Glorybox and the other bands you mentioned are Christian, but I wonder how many friends you have that don't belong to that environment, because you usually find them in clusters. I have often thought about the quote 'also today there is reason to be thankful',[3] not knowing quite who to thank or what for? To be honest, the way you come across does not support my preconceptions about Christians. I guess it's probably more of an inner thing. Although I like you very much, I also admit that we do not know each other too well, and therefore I have had limited time to form opinions on your way of living. It's not that I haven't tried, I have, but I have not had the opportunities to do so fully.

Confused and spinning mostly because my head has been full of thoughts while I've been at your house. To think at one point I avoided these questions at all costs, and now I am willingly trying to find the answers to them. In any case, it's not you who has confused me; it's been mostly my own doing. Long forgotten or perhaps repressed thoughts have suddenly sprung to life.

With regard to overstepping boundaries, I could never imagine offending you in that respect. I consider that very positive. Thanks for the offer of the books. I would very much like to read them; the books I have read lately have swung wildly between quality and content. However, it is a big responsibility to read an objective book on belief in God. I can't be bothered to read a book about the thoughts I form myself. Neither can I be bothered to read a book written by those types who only have time to voice their scorn or disdain for others.

By the way, what did you mean that you don't always maintain your relationship with God ['to me fellowship with him is to see the alpha and omega in daily life'] as well as you should? I forgot to ask that earlier.

Stine

– – –

From: Mikael R. Andreasen
Sent: November 21, 2002 11:44 pm
To: Stine Forsberg
Subject: Re:

Hello again and again and again,

I will attempt to answer/comment on the things in your last email. Yes, I do have groups of friends who belong to 'that' environment, and they are all amazing people. I also have a large group of friends who do not share my beliefs which I consider very important. I would hate to become complacent and stuck in my own way of thinking, which I fear could happen if I were only surrounded by like-minded people. So, thanks to people like you for being there. 'Also today there is reason to be thankful' is not directly aimed at God. I think of it more as an attitude to live by; to be a person who is grateful has to be one of the highest aims in life. To be thankful for the small things too, things that seem inconsequential. A good example is my friend Emil from the band Serena Maneesh. He is always so thankful and humble when you meet him. It's really inspiring to be around people like that. They seem a lot richer in some ways. Does that make sense?

I am unsure how to react to your comments about my appearance not giving away my faith, or beliefs. If I have managed to avoid coming across as the stereotypical Christian, then thank you. Not, however, if my actions or signals have somehow contradicted what I believe. I'm glad that you showed a positive interest in the two books I mentioned. They truly are two exceptional books – even for those who don't believe (I assume so anyway).

Now, on to another of your questions. You asked, 'What do you mean by saying you don't always maintain your relationship with God as well as you should?' Good question. Initially the answer would be that it happens when I prioritise other things higher than him, and that happens time and time again. Although it's not my intention, I end up occupying myself with hundreds of other things and God is left on the back-burner. It's not that I reject and turn away from everything I believe in, but more that God sometimes becomes secondary in my life to other things. On a deeper level it has something to do with a wrong perception of sin that non-Christians often have a difficult time with. Any elaboration on that would best be saved for a proper conversation, it could become too complicated. I don't know how you understand the concept of sin, but if I had to arrive at a conclusion, then I'm sure you see it differently than I do (if you even have an opinion on it). So, remember to ask me about it next time we meet. ☺

Something completely different I just remembered is that I haven't complimented you on your writing style. I am not talking about the last few emails with these deep conversations, more about the shorter 'mini-mails' that you send. I don't know how to explain, but I think you have a simple and great way of expressing yourself.

To think that it's already the weekend again tomorrow. This week has simply flown past, and I can't say I object!

Ciao,

– mik –

- - -

From: Stine Forsberg
Sent: November 22, 2002 0:37 am
To: Mikael R. Andreasen
Subject: Re:

Hi again and again and again . . .

I'm going to have to stop sending these emails to you soon. They are getting so long and take up so much space. I keep them a while in the outbox before sending them off to you, but as they fly to you they are followed by a veil of wise words. I agree completely about how having a positive outlook enriches peoples' lives. That must be universal, whether God exists or not. I try to have a positive outlook, and am very thankful to be alive, and to be surrounded by so many wonderful people. Sometimes I take credit for that! He he . . . no . . . not really . . . I don't really thank anyone. I don't really concern myself with destiny. I guess to some extent I have connected the two. I want to be in charge of my own life, so that pretty much cancels out destiny being the deciding factor and, to an extent, that of a personal God. I know it's incredibly naïve, but I have been subjected to some extremely painful things in my life. I have also been responsible for hurting other people and, in turn, been on the receiving end. Therefore, regardless of how childish a thought it must seem, I have comforted myself in the knowledge that God cannot exist; otherwise such things would never happen in life. In all honesty, I have to admit that the argument does not hold water, it's just an easy lifeline to cling to.

It was exactly that – as you yourself put forward – *that* was the reason I described how your appearance does not seem stereotypically Christian. I have surprised myself. However, I can't be sure that my spontaneous response is correct. To which degree does the criteria for my opinions base itself around real facts or merely prejudices?

One day I remember thinking: 'if only you were the sum of all my preconceptions on Christians, then my prejudices would be justified and everything would be so easy'. I would be released from any fault in not considering the possibility that being a Christian was any different to how I imagined it. By saying so, I am not suggesting that you have shown any digression from what I have come to expect of a believer. So by no means should you be concerned. ☺ On the topic of sin, I would agree that we probably have very different viewpoints. I have never quite understood it from your side. ☺

But now I'm off to bed. I have the luxury of a meeting later than usual tomorrow, but I think I will get up at my normal time and just enjoy being able to enjoy it.

Stine

– – –

From: Mikael R. Andreasen
Sent: November 25, 2002 0:44 am
To: Stine Forsberg
Subject: Re:

Hey Stine,

Are you coming to Loppen on Friday?

Mikael

– – –

From: Stine Forsberg
Sent: November 25, 2002 6:19 am
To: Mikael R. Andreasen
Subject: Re:

Morning!

You are probably still asleep, but there are still a few
of us who have to force ourselves to get up early on a
Monday morning to go to work. ☺ I'm definitely coming
on Friday. For some odd reason I always seem to miss
Glorybox when they play live, so it will be good to
finally catch them. You must be looking forward to it
too.

Hope you had a good weekend.

Stine

– – –

From: Mikael R. Andreasen
Sent: November 25, 2002 10:51 am
To: Stine Forsberg
Subject: Re:

Great that you're coming on Friday.

I was out practising with Glorybox yesterday since they have decided to add an extra guitarist on their opening number. It's going to be fun to play, plus I get in for free.

I heard you ran into my friend David at the Bright Eyes concert? He said the show was amazing.

OK, that's enough for now; I have to record some guitar tracks.

A warm smile from here!

Mikael

– – –

From: Stine Forsberg
Sent: November 25, 2002 3:10 pm
To: Mikael R. Andreasen
Subject: Re:

Now I have an added reason to be excited about the show!

I met David. Apparently both of us had walked around

nervously wondering whether to approach each other or not. I wasn't totally sure it was him either. The concert really was fantastic. It was a unique experience to see him live. The show was probably no longer than a regular concert, but it felt like it lasted longer, a beautiful eternity. Today has been great; everyone has been asking me why I'm so happy. I guess it's just one of those days . . .

All that's good – and a little more.

Stine

– – –

From: Mikael R. Andreasen
Sent: November 25, 2002 3:42 pm
To: Stine Forsberg
Subject: Re:

I'm glad that your day has been so good. I haven't been outside at all today, barely outside my room. Just been sitting recording music all day.

Good afternoon – and now back to recording . . .

Mikael

From: Stine Forsberg
Sent: November 25, 2002 4:15 pm
To: Mikael R. Andreasen
Subject: Re:

I don't think I'll be leaving the house again today. I'm about to pack all my books up in a huge box. It's probably going to weigh a ton, but I don't want to think about that right now . . . I'm just pleased I'm getting it done.

Isn't it bizarre how when you're mulling something over, something personal, then suddenly other things happen that seem to point exactly to those things you were thinking about, yet you'd told no one about them? Strange way of explaining it, I know. But it's weird; today I got a letter from my old religion teacher in high school. He enclosed two old books about Christianity and different forms of relationships with God. Apparently he was clearing out his house, found the books and remembered his sweet pupil. ☺ I used to think a lot about faith, belief, etc. in school and had a lot of discussions with him. Regardless of that, it is weird, that was a long time ago. I almost get the feeling that someone is watching over me. ☺

Stine

- - -

From: Mikael R. Andreasen
Sent: November 26, 2002 7:29 pm
To: Stine Forsberg
Subject: Re:

Hi there,

It's funny how your religion teacher thought of giving you those books.

I was considering coming by tomorrow to drop off the two books I'm lending you. I have to go out and practise with Glorybox so I will be in the area. Is that OK with you?

– mik –

- - -

From: Stine Forsberg
Sent: November 26, 2002 7:51 pm
To: Mikael R. Andreasen
Subject: Re:

I'm going over to help pack some things for the girl I am moving in with. We are hoping to move our things into the apartment over the weekend, so I won't be in tomorrow. I'm not doing anything at the moment, so I could easily ride over and collect the books. That's if you have time and are at home, obviously? I actually need to get some milk anyway.

Stine

– – –

From: Mikael R. Andreasen
Sent: November 26, 2002 8:05 pm
To: Stine Forsberg
Subject: Re:

Hmm, a friend of mine is visiting at the moment, so I haven't got time to be social. You're more than welcome to come by to collect the books, though, it's up to you.

– mik –

– – –

From: Stine Forsberg
Sent: November 26, 2002 8:40 pm
To: Mikael R. Andreasen
Subject: Re:

OK, I've just convinced Anne Mette to come out for a ride with me. I'll drop by at some point. In any case . . . we're leaving now.

– – –

From: Mikael R. Andreasen
Sent: November 26, 2002 11:15 pm
To: Stine Forsberg
Subject: Re:

A quick hello,

I'm sorry that I couldn't be a better host, but Christian was here and bla bla bla . . .

See you on Friday.

Mikael

_ _ _

From: Stine Forsberg
Sent: November 27, 2002 6:50 pm
To: Mikael R. Andreasen
Subject: Re:

Yeah, what kind of treatment was that! No, only joking, don't worry about it. It was only me coming to disturb you. I hope you had a nice evening and that the rest of the day will be great.

Stine

_ _ _

From: Stine Forsberg
Sent: November 27, 2002 10:26 pm
To: Mikael R. Andreasen
Subject: Re:

I'm having such a hard time closing my eyes tonight. Perhaps it's the fact that they are occupied with a very, very good book, or they simply can't find the strength to sleep yet. I've started on the Philip Yancey book. Many thoughts have been set in motion.

Stine

— — —

From: Mikael R. Andreasen
Sent: November 27, 2002 0:52 am
To: Stine Forsberg
Subject: Re:

I'm excited to hear your reactions to the book. It's been a couple of years since I read it so perhaps I should refresh my memory so that I'm able to handle any possible questions you may have. I can't commit to that right now, though, as the clock moves closer and closer to six when the alarm is set.

Take care.

Mikael

— — —

From: Mikael R. Andreasen
Sent: November 28, 2002 11:43 pm
To: Stine Forsberg
Subject: Re:

Hey Stine,

Just checking if you want to be on the guest list at the

Glorybox show tomorrow? I was supposed to put a friend of mine from Jutland on, but he won't be turning up. If you want to be put on the list, then reply soon.

You have probably gone to bed already, but if I don't hear from you before tomorrow evening I will find someone else. I hope that's fine!

Bye,

Mikael

– – –

From: Stine Forsberg
Sent: November 28, 2002 11:48 pm
To: Mikael R. Andreasen
Subject: Re:

Hi Mikael,

You know what? You're almost too good to be true. Thank you so much, I would really appreciate it.

I've been making sweets this afternoon with a friend of mine.

They've turned out really well. Right now there's some honey-nougat setting on the windowsill. I'll be sure to put some aside for you . . .

Stine

– – –

From: Mikael R. Andreasen
Sent: November 28, 2002 11:54 pm
To: Stine Forsberg
Subject: Re:

All right, I'll put you on the list.

– – –

From: Stine Forsberg
Sent: November 30, 2002 3:36 am
To: Mikael R. Andreasen
Subject: Re:

Dearest Mikael,

That was a great concert, thank you so much. It's a shame that the vocals were not loud enough, but it was beautiful . . . beautiful.

I hope you had a great night. It's quite strange meeting again after our email relationship has taken so many twists and turns. It makes it quite nerve-racking to actually meet in person!

Best wishes,

Stine

– – –

From: Mikael R. Andreasen
Sent: November 30, 2002 8:18 pm
To: Stine Forsberg
Subject: Re:

Was it the tour 7″ with Rivulets, Jessica Bailiff and Drekka that you had?!

I'm listening to it right now and it's *good, good, good*! Go buy a record player!

Mikael

– – –

From: Stine Forsberg
Sent: November 30, 2002 8:32 pm
To: Mikael R. Andreasen
Subject: Re:

Ask God to bless me with a record player. ☺ No, I don't have one, I know, it's shameful. For example, I have that tour 7″ lying here which I'll probably never listen to. Ah. (Yes, it's the same 7″ as yours.)

– – –

From: Mikael R. Andreasen
Sent: November 30, 2002 9:18 pm
To: Stine Forsberg
Subject: Re:
Attachment: 7″ tour EP – side aa.mp3 (5,85mb)

Unfortunately, God had no more record players in his store room. However, he did know someone who could transfer the beautiful music to mp3-files. I was asked, for now, to send you these files. The recording is quite faint since it's from vinyl, etc., etc. Just turn it up, or even better put on some headphones. Then sit yourself down, and enjoy it in silence.

– mik –

– – –

From: Stine Forsberg
Sent: November 30, 2002 10:02 pm
To: Mikael R. Andreasen
Subject: Re:

Thank you so, so, so much! The EP is gorgeous. Say hello to God and tell him he is lucky to know that guy-who-knows-how-to-copy-mp3-files, in more ways than one. But, I'm sure God already knows that.

– – –

From: Mikael R. Andreasen
Sent: November 30, 2002 10:40 pm
To: Stine Forsberg
Subject: Re:

God smiled and mumbled something about you having been too vague in your description of that guy-with-the-mp3-files. He did, however, say that he loved him. Speaking of which, I just started thinking about the title of the new Half-handed Cloud record (I'm sure you haven't heard about them); it's called, 'We Haven't Just Been Told, We Have Been Loved'. Aargh, why didn't I come up with that title?!

On the subject of God, a few years ago I made a Christmas calendar where I asked twenty-four young people to write a piece with the title 'God and I'. A text for every day. Hanna, who played Moog and glockenspiel at the show yesterday, wrote the following piece:

God and I
What should I say about us, God? That we delight ourselves in each other? That you, in your overwhelming love, spontaneously surprise me with creative reminders of you. Because you love, and love to bring joy. That all I can do is receive. And give myself to you. Give my love through all I am and all I do. And you tell me it's enough. That it's, everything. If I love you with all my heart, all my soul and all my strength.

Shall I tell about the times you feel so removed? Although you never are, because you have promised to stay. That you teach me through all things and draw me closer to you. That I am learning you are in control. That you give me the will to do good, and give me the strength to be able to. That you don't just say 'come' but show me the way too. That you surround me, are in me. That there is rest in you.

Shall I tell of how nature sings to you? That sometimes bubbling, childish, joy-filled songs drive me to sing and dance . . . rejoicing. That at times there are deep, inner praises, at times silent wonder. All of nature worships you. And I sing along. For your mercy, when I go against your will, your faithfulness, when I am all but faithful, your love gives reason too. Because you are the reason. That you also sing enthusiastic songs to me. That I can bring joy to you.

Shall I tell of your holiness and unfathomable greatness? How you fill me with awe. You are so big, so beautiful, so . . . God. How I might have stood at a distance in amazement and rejoiced over your dignity and holiness. But you kneel down. You ask me how I am doing. You attentively watch over me all day. You breathe on my wounds and relieve me of my burdens. You show me how things should be done.

Shall I tell of how you love me so much, so much that you allow me to know you. That you allow me to explore your personality. That you share your thoughts with me. There is so much more of you. You are unfathomable. And that in itself is wonderful – I can never figure you out. And yet you are unchangeable. Shall I tell of . . . No, they can find out for themselves and further tell.

Now I want to go exploring in you, and with you.

Come.

I simply love the way she writes and I'm so grateful to be her friend. Now I'll have the chicken sandwich that I have just bought!

– – –

From: Stine Forsberg
Sent: November 30, 2002 11:15 pm
To: Mikael R. Andreasen
Subject: Re:

Catch God for a second and ask him to elaborate – why was I too vague?

Doesn't God wonder why you use time and energy on someone who doesn't even believe that he is there? Huh?

And what exactly does it mean that God speaks to us? In what way exactly does he give comfort and encouragement when you need it? What is it to be filled with God's love? And what does it mean to receive answers from him when you ask? (You can understand now that twenty questions have come to mind for the professor . . . ☺)

But really, these things are far too abstract for me to understand.

It was an interesting piece; I think I read it through three times before small fragments began to give some sort of meaning. I guess that's to be expected when words and notions that your friend mentions – also in that context – are relatively new to me.

It's great that the first of December is tomorrow. I don't really have a Christmas calendar so I am looking forward to you sending me your entry from 'God and I'. I'm sure you can find time to send it.

— — —

From: Mikael R. Andreasen
Sent: November 30, 2002 11:55 pm
To: Stine Forsberg
Subject: Re:

He didn't really want to elaborate, about the vagueness. I think it had something to do with my shortcomings. No, I'm ranting now. I am sure, though, that he is far happier that I spend time with someone who doesn't believe in him rather than someone who does. Such is my God.

You ask good questions. They are not easy to reply to. Should I try? Hmm . . . OK.

That God 'speaks to us' is an expression most Christians would use, but exactly what it means, or furthermore how God speaks to us, is a very individual thing. For me it's primarily that I believe he, at times, puts things into my thoughts, sometimes completely out of the blue. One concrete example was a time when I thought he said something to me about a friend. It was something about her situation in life. They were things I, normally, had no reason to say to her, but I believed that they were from God and I went and said them to her. She began to cry, because they were the exact things she needed to hear at that time in her life. That was a strange experience.

I think that experience also helps answer your next question. Sometimes God uses other people to bring comfort and encouragement to us when it's needed. An unexpected phone call, a letter, someone who surprises you with something, I don't know. I do also believe that he himself can bring comfort and encouragement. Here's where it perhaps becomes abstract. But he can suddenly give you an extreme feeling of being loved and accepted. I can't really put it into words, but it's amazing. It's almost as though it goes deeper than feelings and understanding. In that feeling of being accepted and loved, you find peace. That peace gives you enough to also reach out to others. Ah, I think I'm mixing my words now and that in trying to answer your questions separately I have somehow jumbled them all together.

Now the question about how God answers us when we ask him questions.

Hmm . . . you should probably ask Jan from Glorybox if you happen to talk to him one day. He can tell you some crazy things that have happened to them. For the first two years the band were living in the same apartment that Jan-Erik and Mai now live in. They had no jobs and claimed no state benefits since they believed that God wanted them to spend time playing music. In that way they lived by faith, trusting that God would provide for their everyday needs. And he did. The rent was paid, food was laid out on the table. On top of that, they received most of their equipment as presents from all sorts of strange people. One example was when they were about to play their first concert and needed transport. A couple of days before the show a complete stranger called them and said he had a trailer that he was about to throw out, but just wondered if anyone needed it. The amount of similar stories I have heard about, or seen, assures me that they are not coincidences.

Feel free to point out if my answers don't measure up.

My submission to 'God and I' was not especially good, but I will send it later (after midnight).

Here are some other words that I really like:

Often it's the small things
that make a difference.
To others,
a seemingly inconsequential
or overlooked detail.
Something that shouldn't be
attributed any value,
yet to you,
becomes exceedingly valuable.
Perhaps that's the manner
in which another person
expresses a particular
word.

DECEMBER 2002

From: Stine Forsberg
Sent: December 01, 2002 0:37 am
To: Mikael R. Andreasen
Subject: Re:

As I sit here having read your wonderful email, with
small bitter tears running down my cheeks, is it
because (a possibly existing) God has chosen to place
you in my life, for my sake? Do you think God select-
ively chooses people to place into others' lives so that
things suddenly find meaning? To shepherd them along
the way? Perhaps because he knows they have a need
for it? Does it work both ways? Is it solely because he
thinks I have a need for your wisdom and beliefs? I
guess now it's me who is rambling . . . You will have to
take into consideration – as you read what I write –
that I, in your eyes, probably haven't opened mine yet.
Also, just realise that I really cannot find anything valid
inside me that would make me cling to the idea that I

am a child of God, etc. Therefore, I am probably asking a lot of stupid questions.

I completely understand what you mean about the not-too-coincidental-coincidences. You use some beautiful examples, so intense. I myself have played with the thought lately, because I have felt myself caught off-guard by something. OK, I've met you and I am learning a lot. Almost everywhere I turn I end up in a discussion, sometimes about the earth's origins in the back of a bus, or with teachers at school. Big questions are thrown into the air one after another, and I want to grasp them all. Before, I would have felt totally confused and depressed. Then there's my old religion teacher, who completely out of the blue sent me the two books, both of which contain the following sentence inside the cover: 'from an old teacher with the hope of new understanding'. At the book exhibition one of the lectures I was supposed to attend was moved, but I didn't know. So I sat myself down with the expectancy of listening to Jakob Ejersbo, but instead began a study arranged by the Anis publishers entitled 'How can I know God exists if I don't believe in him?' Strange . . . strange . . .

I thought the answers you came up with were fantastic, overwhelming in more ways than one. I have no idea how to respond to the last words you wrote about *the small things*; they were just so beautiful . . .

When you get the opportunity, try to go back to the questions about sin. When is it that you, for example, feel you are not loyal or keeping your end of the deal in relation to God?

In short, are you rewarded by commission? That the more helpless, poor souls you take under your wing, the more calls and care you get handed on a plate from God? No . . . that was just for fun, ignore it.

– – –

From: Mikael R. Andreasen
Sent: December 01, 2002 0:59 am
To: Stine Forsberg
Subject: Re:

Dear Stine,

Thank you so much for your email. It was so honest, which I loved, and it was also a vote of confidence. I want to stress (once again) that I never want you to feel as though I am pressurising you or force-feeding you with answers. That I think you are a great person has nothing to do with whether you find God or not. The crazy thing with God is that he loves us all regardless of whether we believe in him or not. Obviously that's something I believe, but it's one of those things I just love about him. He is so illogical in many ways. The ways in which he acts are so contradictory to human beings that I find it absurd to believe he is a product of our imagination. It would be a ridiculous God to invent. I laughed when I read what you wrote about commission. This afternoon I have been gripped by nostalgia, sitting with headphones on reading old letters and documents on my computer. While rifling around I also found the small text I had written about how it's often the little things that make the most impact. Well, I had actually just finished reading another old text when your email popped up. It seemed to coincide with your joke about being rewarded on a commission basis, so you'll have to read it.

Do you like gravy?

It was a family party a few years ago – and a pleasure to see them all again. Add to this an abundant family meal and a decent wine. Ideal settings. After a filling main course and dessert, and while awaiting the coffee, we passed the time, mainly in the sun-drenched garden. Not me. I chose to go out to the kitchen to rinse the dishes. The almost empty gravy jugs needed some water. As I stood rinsing them I thought to myself that it's only a matter of time before I get gravy stains on my shirt. It would be typical of me to have such an accident. A second later I relaxed. 'When you do a good deed, and especially of your own initiative, accidents don't happen. There is a higher power that guarantees it,' I thought.

Quite rightly, nothing happened.

Nevertheless I felt down. Down because I had actually allowed myself to think such an idiotic thought. Not idiotic in the sense that I truly believed a higher power sat and steered the contents of a gravy jug; idiotic because I had fallen into the line of thinking that if I do something good, I expect something good in return – or at least for nothing bad to happen. How I longed to be rid of that thought. It popped up periodically and irritated me no end. Oh God, I helped that old lady, so now I pray that you will do such and such. The examples are endless. But it shall not continue! I hope that need in itself shouts so loud that I am drawn to it and learn completely what it is to meet others' needs as a blessing. Even if it ends up costing me something. Perhaps I should have spilled gravy on myself?

I'll send the mail now. I'll try to comment on the other things in your email in a little while.

So long,

– mik –

– – –

From: Stine Forsberg
Sent: December 01, 2002 1:11 am
To: Mikael R. Andreasen
Subject: Re:

What a thoroughly fun text!

It got me thinking about the time my parents got divorced, a long time ago, when I prayed to God. The first, and only, time. I was so sad and remember thinking: Dear God, I have never asked you for anything before so I think it only reasonable that you fulfil a wish or two for me. I guess that's the typical way a non-believer relates to a higher power . . . with complete naïveté.

– – –

From: Mikael R. Andreasen
Sent: December 01, 2002 2:05 am
To: Stine Forsberg
Subject: Re:

Hi again. I have written in between your excerpts. Your text is smaller

> As I sit here after having read your wonderful email, with small bitter tears running down my cheeks, is it because (a possibly existing) God has chosen to place you in my life, for my sake? Do you think God selectively chooses people to place into others' lives so that things suddenly find meaning? To shepherd them along the way? Perhaps because he knows they have a need for it?

I am not in any position to calculate how foresighted God is. I also believe in free will, the ability to choose differently from what God wants. I believe just as much in the fact that you run into so many people, and some of them you end up having interesting conversations with. However . . . hmm . . . maybe God does have some odd game up his sleeve. I don't know.

> Does it work both ways? Is it solely because he thinks I have a need for your wisdom and beliefs? I guess now it's me who is rambling . . . You will have to take into consideration – as you read what I write – that I, in your eyes, probably haven't opened mine yet. Also, just realise that I really cannot find anything valid inside me that would make me cling to the idea that I am a child of God, etc. Therefore, I am probably asking a lot of stupid questions.

It's always embarrassing to rely on clichés, but I really mean that there are no dumb questions to be asked. I think yours are good and sensible.

> I completely understand what you mean about the not-too-coincidental-coincidences. You use some beautiful examples, so intense. I myself have played with the thought lately, because I have felt myself caught off-guard by something. OK, I've met you and I am learning a lot. Almost everywhere I turn I end up in a discussion, sometimes about the earth's origins in the back of a bus, or with teachers at school. Big questions are thrown into the air one after another, and I want to grasp them all. Before, I would have felt totally confused and depressed. Then there's my old religion teacher, who completely out of the blue sent me the two books, both of which contain the following sentence inside the cover: 'from an old teacher with the hope of new understanding'. At the book exhibition one of the lectures I was supposed to attend was moved, but I didn't know. So I sat myself down with the expectancy of listening to Jakob Ejersbo, but instead began a study arranged by the Anis publishers entitled 'How can I know God exists if I don't believe in him?' Strange . . . strange . . .

Yeah, there are many strange 'coincidences'. I would, however, never build my faith on them. If I didn't believe in God and Jan came over to me and told me all his stories about this and that, it wouldn't be enough to make me believe. Faith is a quantity that regardless of situation must be believed in or not. It's exactly that which defines faith – that you cannot just open a book and read 'God exists'. My point being that in life there are many instances of 'coincidence', and these coincidences in themselves prove nothing, but when you believe, these 'coincidences' take on new meanings. But why is it that God doesn't just show himself? Why doesn't he stand on a cloud somewhere and say: 'Hey, here I am. You can see for yourselves that I exist, nobody can deny that now.'

My answer would be that God doesn't want to have fellowship with us in that way. I completely believe that God is love, and that his designs for love are ideal. Therefore he only seeks fellowship with those who, having free will, seek him (and find him) – and not because he has positioned himself up on a cloud so that nobody can reject him. He wants fellowship because we too have sought it.

> I thought the answers you came up with were fantastic, overwhelming in more ways than one. I have no idea how to respond to the last words you wrote about *the small things*; they were just so beautiful . . .

Thanks (I'm blushing). I can't remember when I wrote them (the last words) and in which context. Perhaps they just appeared one day.

> When you get the opportunity, try to go back to the questions about sin. When is it that you, for example, feel you are not loyal or keeping your end of the deal in relation to God?

It's a hefty thing you are asking me to explain here. My starting point would be that God is, and has created. He longs for fellowship with people. I believe that in his creation he has an ideal of how things should be. This includes how the relationship between God and man should be. Sin is where we break out of the ideal that God has for us. I think it can be put that simply. That sin, in essence, is people missing out on the ideals that God has for them. Does that make sense?

Sin is not about rules and regulations. It's more a question of how things are in our relationship to God. There are things that can eventually enter in and break that relationship. I have spoken a lot about this with another non-Christian friend of mine. The point where he turns away in regards to Christianity is its failure to accept homosexuality. He isn't a homosexual himself, but cannot understand why a homosexual relationship cannot be as loving and beautiful as a heterosexual one. He thinks Christians are very judgmental in that area. There are many Christians who would judge someone for being gay, and I apologise for that! I would never judge a gay person, but I still believe that it is sin. That must be taken in the context of my way of explaining sin.

As Mikael, the person, I can completely understand how Lisa's and Amy's relationship can be just as beautiful as Susan's and Andy's. Lisa and Amy could very well prove to be better parents than Susan and Andy. Yet, I still claim that it is sin, because I believe ideally God has made man and woman to be together. Then follows the question of how I follow God's ideals and thoughts in my own life? I don't believe I would be following them if I married Neil. Can you follow my trail of thought? Since I have a relationship with God based on mutual love, I don't want to hurt him or disappoint him, so I obviously would love to aim for the ideals he has laid out for me. Seen like that, sin no longer has the suffocating character that is so often portrayed. It's not a straight-jacket. It only describes a situation where I miss the ideals that God has laid out for me.

Wow, that turned into a long tirade, and I wrote myself out on a tangent. As I said earlier, I would like to talk about this whole consciousness of sin in person sometime.

In response to your question about when I feel I have been disloyal in my relationship to God:

I feel that I let God down when I am, for example, arrogant. And, believe me, I can be arrogant. I don't want to be, but it's a trait that often slips out unexpectedly. I also feel it when I ignore people who have a need. Also, when I talk behind people's backs. When I . . .

I could reel sentences off for eternity. But no, it's not about a long list of things I cannot do because it would result in God not loving me. God loves us all regardless. Despite what I do, or don't do, I can come 'home' to God and know that I'm loved. Though sometimes I do need to apologise to him, to rekindle the relationship I have with him. In reality it's about a loving relationship, more than anything.

Anyway, there's a band called Soul Junk, have I told you about them? The lead singer, called Glen Galaxy, used to play in Trumans Water. He found God and started the band Soul Junk (he still apparently plays with Trumans Water). Soul Junk write some insane music, and on their website they have an explanation of what they're 'all about'. I just happened to think about it while I wrote about the love relationship we can have with God. Here goes:

The great failure of all 'religion' is that it cannot get to your insides. It's like a mould to fit yourself into – it changes your shape, but does nothing for your spirit. So the world looks on and rejects it as plastic and external – a band-aid for the open soul. Consider the possibility tonight that what you've rejected is not God; it's man's attempt to play God. Please allow us to worship the one we call our God openly in front of you tonight. We do this with a deep respect for your own spiritual understanding and honesty. We ask that our Jesus would demonstrate the inner truth of these words – that God is a spirit and we worship him in spirit and truth. Let us provide a soundtrack of reconciliation for you. Especially be willing to sense our God's presence, since this is the possibility and reality that shatters external religion and actually touches the spirit. We sing peace to those far and near in the name of Jesus. Welcome to the evening's pyrotechnics of spirit and sound – shadows, sheets, pictures pointing to and worshipping the one who inspires, who breathes life, who is life. We sing into a decade that champions a nameless spirituality; that acknowledges the transcendent, the infinite, the eternal – but has chosen not to name it as the fashion. We play with openness in mind – naming the one we worship but not judging those with other views. We invite the Holy Spirit of our God to fall on us as we play, and by doing so announce the existence of a new peace, a new power, and new sexuality/intimacy – all in the name of the one who calls himself the bridegroom, who comes changing water into wine, as much lover as king. So we invite you to look on, join in, experience our worship, drink the new wine with us, soak up whatever our God chooses to reveal of himself tonight. Then take it apart, examine it, criticise it – and wonder inside whether this could be true – that our God is more about romance than religion, that he exists and is choosing to live inside people who open themselves to him, believe what they know of him and speak his beautiful name Jesus.[4]

Maybe I should send you a song or two by Soul Junk – if only to remove the stereotype that all Christian music is hymns (though they can be beautiful), and awful (in my opinion) gospel music.

In short, are you rewarded by commission? That the more helpless, poor souls you take under your wing, the more calls and care you get handed on a plate from God? No . . . that was just for fun, ignore it.

Actually, I think I already covered this with the text I sent you.

That turned out to be a long email. I am soon heading off to bed. If you want to write any more tonight, it will have to be within the next twenty minutes!

Love,

Mikael

- - -

From: Stine Forsberg
Sent: December 01, 2002 2:25 am
To: Mikael R. Andreasen
Subject: Re:

Just go to bed. I think I'll stay up a bit longer. I still can't believe how you wrote those beautiful words about *the small things*, not because I find it hard to associate you with writing such words, but they really are so lovely. You for one should not be upset at not coming up with the title to that Half-handed Cloud CD . . . nope.

Hmm . . . right now I'm completely blank. There are so many things to think through and reach an opinion on. I think I'll have to sleep on it. Tomorrow I feel like taking a train to Jutland and finding a huge forest to sit in. You should definitely come with . . . no . . . I'm drifting now . . . sorry.

If our correspondence were taken as the subject for an evening class, or an afternoon course, then I would have to say I am very satisfied with the service, and the improving standard! In fact, I would go as far as to say I am ready to sign on for one more term. You can always send an invoice later!

I think it's a fun thing – that you live in a relationship with God . . . May you live long and happily together. ☺ And sleep well, right?!

– – –

From: Mikael R. Andreasen
Sent: December 01, 2002 2:35 am
To: Stine Forsberg
Subject: Re:
Attachment: 05_Soul_Junk_-_Peace_Peace_Peace.mp3
(2,16MB)[5]

Here follows my humble contribution to the Christmas
calendar. I am not really satisfied with it. I feel it doesn't match
up to what I think I am capable of, but who cares . . . here it
is:

Good morning.
See how the sun shines.
It promises to be a good day.
God will be here in a little bit.
We're going to town, God and I.
I don't think we're doing anything specific,
just wander around a little,
watch people,
buy a nice shirt, perhaps.
Yeah, and then we'll obviously go in
and see if any essential albums
have arrived.
When we get hungry I know exactly
where we'll go,
It's apparently my turn to buy.
It will be one of those days
that later on at night
– lying in bed –
you wonder exactly why the day
turned out as it did.

A real let's-see-what-happens-day.
It's a bit embarrassing,
we have planned
this day many many times, God and I,
and each time I have called it off.
There has just been so much else happening.
But today, today we'll have a fun time,
God and I.

Just got your email, and read it quickly. I'm just so tired I will leave it for later. Have a great trip to Jutland, if you go. ☺

I'm attaching a Soul Junk song, one of the more accessible ones. The lyrics are:

Peace peace peace
My peace I leave with you
Not as the world gives
At all

May the song bring peace – in one way or another between the sloppy drumming and almost-in-tune voices. Should be listened to with headphones!

Now, brush teeth . . . bed!

Goodnight,

Mikael

－－－

From: Mikael R. Andreasen
Sent: December 01, 2002 1:38 pm
To: Stine Forsberg
Subject: Re:

Good morning.

I have spent the last one and a half hours mixing and messing around with my digital delay pedal, and now it's about time for a shower.

Heading to church at 3 pm. ☺

Wishing you a good first Sunday of Advent – from someone who doesn't even have an Advent band! ☺

Mikael

－－－

From: Stine Forsberg
Sent: December 01, 2002 2:02 pm
To: Mikael R. Andreasen
Subject: Re:

Your contribution to the Christmas calendar was really good. One thing I really like about you is how you stand firm even in not knowing, that you believe and yet doubt at the same time . . . I think that's great. I also think it's a wonderful proclamation of love . . . I can see why God likes you. ☺

All that talk about sin I find very difficult to relate to. In fact I feel the same way as your friend does about it. Homosexuals can be good Christians, can't they? Are you saying that they would have to wake up every single day and repent for what they are? Is homosexuality what they keep falling into – like when you, as you mentioned before, get wrapped up in your arrogance?

Another thing I thought about as I was falling asleep last night . . . Don't you have a duty to like everybody? (e.g. your words: 'That I think you are a great person has nothing to do with whether you find God or not. The crazy thing with God is that he loves us all regardless of whether we believe in him or not. Obviously that's something I believe, but it's one of those things I just love about him.')

Strange. When night has passed, and the day brightens up the heavens, you can't help but feel a little more transparent, exposed. And on that note I shall take a shower and then ride down to the zoo, to become one with nature.

Pass on my greetings in church . . . and have a wonderful 1st December.

From: Stine Forsberg
Sent: December 01, 2002 8:23 pm
To: Mikael R. Andreasen
Subject: Re:

If you have a TV and were thinking of watching it tonight, then I can recommend a programme tonight at 11 pm. It's called *The Obedience Dilemma*, from 1978. It's a great documentary. It's very interesting to observe the victim of authority. An exciting, psychological experiment. I'll be recording it, and I think you should see it one day.

From: Mikael R. Andreasen
Sent: December 02, 2002 2:22 am
To: Stine Forsberg
Subject: Re:

Hi!

No, I didn't watch TV. After church I headed over to Jan and Sarah's house. We made some food, played crazy songs on the guitar and flute, fooled around with names for babies and just enjoyed the fact that it was a Sunday afternoon. I just got home. I am very interested in seeing that programme.

However, it's bedtime now. Have a good day at work tomorrow!

Mikael

– – –

From: Mikael R. Andreasen
Sent: December 02, 2002 8:43 pm
To: Stine Forsberg
Subject: Re:

Hi!

Church was good yesterday. The pastor spoke about the importance of fellowship – how fellowship is something that each of us has a responsibility for, yet it should never compromise or restrict our individuality. He gave us examples from Paul's letters where he spoke of us all being parts of the same body, and that each part is crucial for the whole body to function. That thought is something I value highly, the possibility that everybody has a relevant role, regardless of their function in a fellowship.

Now, concerning the questions about homosexuality: I doubt I can answer this without clashing, or offending you in some way. I think it's impossible to combine a living relationship with God and a homosexual lifestyle. I can see how that could sound rather harsh, and from a neutral standpoint it probably is. However, when your goal is to live inside God's ideals for our lives, then a homosexual relationship is a constant violation of that.

If, for instance, I act in an arrogant way, speak badly about someone else, then in that instance I destroy something in my relationship with God (and with other people). It's then up to me to ask God, and the other people involved, for forgiveness. If you live in a homosexual lifestyle, then it's a constant choice to reject the ideals God has put in place.

Believe me, I can completely understand how this might sound absurd or insane. I think that some homosexual couples can have a far better relationship than some heterosexuals, but when you start knowing God and seeing things from his thoughts and ideals, then things look a little different.

On the other hand, I hate it when Christians end up in social debates against, for example, homosexuals. I find it unfair to expect non-Christians to understand the Christian view that homosexuality is wrong. If someone first comes to know God, and that inevitably means that some things have to change in their life, then that can come later. I know a guy who chose to live a gay lifestyle, and felt that he had to desert God. He simply couldn't find peace combining the two. Do you understand?

If Christianity was only based on being a charitable person, etc., then I could see no problem in a gay person being a good Christian.

However, that's not what Christianity is about at all. The basis is to find and nurture a relationship with God, in which he has set up some boundaries. In return he has given us the freedom to end the relationship, nothing is forced. I, personally, am glad that there are some boundaries, because I think it's impossible to be free unless there are a few. If there were no boundaries at all, then everything would be blasé and freedom would be an illusion.

Is it my duty to think everyone's nice, you ask. Ha ha, funny question!

I don't think that's my duty, although I do think I should try to treat everyone as my neighbour. To try and meet them in a loving and obliging way. And no, I don't always succeed, especially when my arrogance comes knocking.

Stine, I can't manage to write any more right now. I have drunk some strong mulled wine and feel rather drowsy. I hung out with Jan today in town. Among other things we headed down to Baden-Baden to buy some CDs at half price! I'm off now, to drink some milk and eat something.

Bye,

Mikael

– – –

From: Stine Forsberg
Sent: December 02, 2002 10:40 pm
To: Mikael R. Andreasen
Subject: Re:

Hi Mikael,

I have just come in the door after a long, long day in the real world. I still haven't picked up my bike, even though it was the only real mission I had all weekend. However, public transport has allowed me the luxury of getting through many pages in one of the books – the one by Yancey – that you lent me. I have been slightly overwhelmed and will definitely contradict myself a lot in this email. I suppose it's only natural when ignorance has set boundaries for one's earlier perception of the world's workings. I am in no way embarrassed to admit that I have been horribly wrong in many areas. I really don't want to bother you with that right now, because there are so many things flying around in my head that you will almost certainly not be able to understand what I mean with it all. I don't want to confuse you any more than necessary! I am inhaling the book whole, believe me. Thanks for lending it to me. There have been some chapters that I have had trouble understanding, although I don't know if it's simply the differences between you and me that cause it. What I mean is that I might not be able to understand it since I'm not a believer. A few things have also made me feel rather upset.

I've been thinking that perhaps it's not a lack of desire that causes me to doubt. I just don't think I can believe . . . is it a weak excuse to call it a matter of habit? You have most likely grown up in a very Christian home – which has without doubt contributed to your upbringing and current outlook on life. I know it's cowardly to say that. Deep down inside I know that it's not true.

I almost fell in love with Jesus in the passage where Philip Yancey speaks about how he would have reacted if he had followed and observed Jesus in his time . . . I have friends who would think I've gone insane if I mentioned that in front of them. ☺

No, I promised myself just a minute ago not to submit you to my bipolar nature. But anyway – it really is a fantastic book which is even beneficial to a non-believer. I am just sorry that I've almost finished it. Have you, by any chance, read John Milton's *Paradise Lost* or *Paradise Regained*? Philip Yancey uses excerpts from both of them in his second chapter, 'Birth: the earth gets visitors'. He just uses some gorgeous passages.

This afternoon I went out to eat at Bryggen with a friend of mine who has two cute sons. August, the oldest one, had been given some money, and with cash in hand had gone to a shop and bought twenty-four boxes for me which he meticulously packed in red silk paper. A box calendar. It was incredibly sweet, and I was so touched when he gave them to me. Inside today's box he had written, in childish handwriting: 'I like you a lot'. He is so sweet. Inside the box was a white angel which is now hanging by my bed. With regard to the talk about nice people, my need for approval must be one of the most terrible things about not having something or someone greater than yourself that cares for you . . . oh, that sounded silly. I think I need some of that strong wine you had yesterday, but I have to make do with tea!

God bless! Ha ha, yeah, why not?! ☺

Stine

– – –

From: Stine Forsberg
Sent: December 02, 2002 11:09 pm
To: Mikael R. Andreasen
Subject: Re:

Oh, I forgot to add (not that I feel obliged to) that on the way home by bus I got an explanation, from the sympathetic Philip Yancey, about the benefits of firm boundaries as opposed to unlimited freedom. Funny how you just mentioned that in your email too.

Ah, I just burned my tongue on far too hot Christmas tea!

– – –

From: Mikael R. Andreasen
Sent: December 02, 2002 11:45 pm
To: Stine Forsberg
Subject: Re:

Hi Stine. I have commented a little further down on your email. Your bits are in smaller text:

Hi Mikael,

I have just come in the door after a long, long day in the real world. I still haven't picked up my bike, even though it was the only real mission I had all weekend. However, public transport has allowed me the luxury of getting through many pages in one of the books – the one by Yancey – that you lent me. I have been slightly overwhelmed and will definitely contradict myself a lot in this email. I suppose it's only natural when ignorance has set boundaries for one's earlier perception of the world's workings. I am in no way embarrassed to admit that I have been horribly wrong in many areas. I really don't want to bother you with that right now, because there are so many things flying around in my head that you will almost certainly not be able to understand what I mean with it all. I don't want to confuse you any more than necessary! I am inhaling the book whole, believe me. Thanks for lending it to me. There have been some chapters that I have had trouble understanding, although I don't know if it's simply the differences between you and me that cause it. What I mean is that I might not be able to understand it since I'm not a believer.

I would like to hear what it is you don't think you understand. The fact that you contradict yourself definitely doesn't warrant an apology. Also, by all means be confused. Confusion is a great state to be in.

A few things have also made me feel rather upset.

I'm curious to hear more about this, but don't feel obliged to say any more than you are comfortable with.

I've been thinking that perhaps it's not a lack of desire that causes me to doubt. I just don't think I can believe . . . is it a weak excuse to call it a matter of habit? You have most likely grown up in a very Christian home – which has without doubt contributed to your upbringing and current outlook on life. I know it's cowardly to say that. Deep down inside I know that it's not true.

Yes, I did grow up in a Christian home, where both my parents believe in God. My mother also grew up in a Christian home, but my dad didn't. He grew up in Copenhagen and one day – on his own initiative – walked into a church in a slightly intoxicated condition and met some Christians who 'took to him'. However, my upbringing was not strict in a religious way. Both my sister and I were given a lot of freedom to choose what we wanted. I hardly ever went to church while I was at high school, not because I had given up on God, but more because of things in the church I could do without. During school I began to think that I could sustain my relationship with God alone, but slowly he became more and more distant and I almost began to ignore him in the end.

I can completely empathise with your opinion that you will never believe. The notion seems so insanely pathetic in many ways. I agree with Søren Kirkegaard when he says it's like throwing yourself out into a bottomless ocean and hoping you float. There are no obvious guarantees. I would add that the most amazing thing is to actually throw yourself out and realise that you're safe. That's strange.

> I almost fell in love with Jesus in the passage where Philip Yancey speaks about how he would have reacted if he had followed and observed Jesus in his time . . . I have friends who would think I've gone insane if I mentioned that in front of them. ☺

I promise not to tell them! ☺

> No, I promised myself just a minute ago not to submit you to my bi-polar nature. But anyway – it really is a fantastic book which is even beneficial to a non-believer. I am just sorry that

I've almost finished it. Have you, by any chance, read John Milton's *Paradise Lost* or *Paradise Regained*? Philip Yancey uses excerpts from both of them in his second chapter, 'Birth: the earth gets visitors'. He just uses some gorgeous passages.

Now comes the surprise that I hadn't considered when I lent you the book. Philip Yancey has also written a book called *What's So Amazing About Grace?*, as well as *The Jesus I Never Knew*. I have this book about grace as well, and you're more than welcome to borrow it. Grace is a wild concept. I once wrote a very short assignment on it. If you want, I can send you my submission. It will offer a short resumé on what the meaning of grace covers. No, I haven't read John Milton – only a few odd quotes here and there.

This afternoon I went out to eat at Bryggen with a friend of mine who has two cute sons. August, the oldest one, had been given some money, and with cash in hand had gone to a shop and bought twenty-four boxes for me which he meticulously packed in red silk paper. A box calendar. It was incredibly sweet, and I was so touched when he gave them to me. Inside today's box he had written, in childish handwriting: 'I like you a lot'. He is so sweet. Inside the box was a white angel which is now hanging by my bed.

That sounds fantastic. Children are so amazing.

With regard to the talk about nice people, my need for approval must be one of the most terrible things about not having something or someone greater than yourself that cares for you . . . oh, that sounded silly.

Hmm . . . that didn't sound silly.

> I think I need some of that strong wine you had yesterday,
> but have to make do with tea!

The mulled wine was from Irma and was deliciously strong, but Jan and I became a bit too drowsy. As we walked around town we were both hoping it was a Friday evening so that we could go and sit in any old pub and drink a nice Christmas beer. Unfortunately, it was a Monday, and at least one of us had to get up the next day at an ungodly hour!

> God bless! Ha ha, yeah, why not?! ☺

Right back at ya!

Mikael

– – –

From: Mikael R. Andreasen
Sent: December 02, 2002 11:47 pm
To: Stine Forsberg
Subject: Re:

Your text again:

> Oh, I forgot to add (not that I feel obliged to) that on the way
> home by bus I got an explanation, from the sympathetic
> Philip Yancey, about the benefits of firm boundaries as
> opposed to unlimited freedom. Funny how you just
> mentioned that in your email too.

He writes about that? Hmm . . . I hadn't thought of that. It has been at least three years since I read the book.

Ah, I just burned my tongue on far too hot Christmas tea!

Poor thing. Now you have to sit and stick your tongue out of the window all night!

— — —

From: Stine Forsberg
Sent: December 03, 2002 0:59 am
To: Mikael R. Andreasen
Subject: Re:

Hi again,

I become so happy every time you email, just so you know. ☺

In your last email there were some things I didn't understand. I wonder if they're too complicated to bring up here. I can try . . .

I am not completely sold on the temptation in the desert story. It seems crystal clear when Philip Yancey describes how Jesus refuses the challenge to show his powers. The point just doesn't sit completely . . . and yet it does. I am slightly unsure. I think I'd better read the passage one more time. Another one I am confused about is the following:

In the mornings, before the sun rose to high

above the hilltops, I went jogging along dirt roads that coiled among the stalky stands of saguaro cacti. Wary of rattlesnakes and scorpions, I mostly kept my head down looking at the road, but one morning on a new route I glanced up to see a shimmering resort looming before me, almost like a mirage. I jogged closer and discovered two Olympic swimming pools, aerobic workout rooms, a cinder jogging trail, lush gardens, a baseball diamond, soccer fields, and horse stables. The facilities, I learned, belonged to a famous eating disorder clinic that caters to movie stars and athletes. The clinic features the latest twelve-step programme techniques, has a staff well stocked with Ph.D.s and M.D.s, and charges its clients about $300 per day.

I jogged slowly back to the jumble of houses and buildings at the Wycliffe base, keenly aware of their contrast to the gleaming architecture of the eating disorder clinic. One institution endeavoured to save souls, to prepare people to serve God here and in eternity, the other endeavoured to save bodies, to prepare people to enjoy this life. It seemed obvious which institution the world honours.

I can completely understand that among other things he doesn't concern himself with over-abundance or excess. Even so, I don't understand it. Also, the point about the eating disorder clinic and the healing of limbs being contrasted to the healing of the soul. That point escaped me, so I looked at it further . . . I am just unsure of his point.

'Blessed are the unfortunate . . .' I don't quite follow that. I have read it again and again – and one place or another I lose track . . . Yet at times I feel I understand it as I am reading the words, but as soon as my eyes lift off the page, it's gone.

I put in the earlier email 'a few things have also made me feel rather upset', and you put 'I'm curious about hearing more on this. Don't feel obliged to say any more than you are comfortable with.'

I surprise myself by making such an effort to understand all of this without, as mentioned, being dissuaded by my own inadequacies – that I make mistakes and learn through them. However, sometimes I think it's unfair how Philip Yancey writes that God's kingdom, which grows amid all evil, is described by Jesus as being wheat growing up among weeds. Difficult to explain. I just think that was a little weak of Jesus . . . as I wrote before, not only for the fact that I haven't found anything inside me to which I can attach the idea that God does exist. I am trying. But to think that I am only part of those weeds – a boring weed that nobody bothers to play with other than other weeds. I sincerely hope I am more than that in *your* eyes. I feel left out sometimes when it comes down to issues of faith, heaven, etc . . . and I am, because ultimately I have chosen to be. I don't know . . . but . . . ah . . . now I don't know what to write any more. This has turned into the worst case of gibberish so far.

I would like to read that assignment that you wrote — as long as you don't mind me reading it.

Preconception number 1 has been quickly thrown aside: I didn't think Christians touched alcohol. Why/why not?

I would like to write a lot more, but I really need to go to bed. The plan is to get up early and go get my bicycle . . . ah . . . why didn't I just do it on Saturday? It would have been so much easier.

Have a nice day at work tomorrow.

Stine

— — —

From: Mikael R. Andreasen
Sent: December 03, 2002 7:54 pm
To: Stine Forsberg
Subject: Re:

Good afternoon!

I will get around to answering your last email, but not now. I am tired and don't have the energy. The children at school have been tiring and I haven't been getting enough sleep lately.

Have a good time.

Mikael

From: Stine Forsberg
Sent: December 03, 2002 8:38 pm
To: Mikael R. Andreasen
Subject: Re:

I've said it many times before (or perhaps just thought it) that you shouldn't do this for my sake – play-act expert on this subject. I can't stand to be a burden . . .

Stine

From: Mikael R. Andreasen
Sent: December 03, 2002 8:51 pm
To: Stine Forsberg
Subject: Re:

Final email from me today. ☺

Stine, you are not a burden – in any way. I find it intensely interesting, and a privilege to be able to get close to someone else's thoughts and conclusions. Thanks!

I do not consider myself an expert in this field at all. I possibly just have the advantage of having been through some of the same thoughts you are having at the moment.

Have a great, great afternoon!

Mikael

From: Mikael R. Andreasen
Sent: December 04, 2002 6:51 pm
To: Stine Forsberg
Subject: Re:

Hi Stine,

I have tried to comment in between excerpts of your email (in smaller text):

> In your last email there were some things I didn't understand. I wonder if they're too complicated to bring up here. I can try . . .

> I am not completely sold on the temptation in the desert story. It seems crystal clear when Philip Yancey describes how Jesus refuses the challenge to show his powers. The point just doesn't sit completely . . . and yet it does. I am slightly unsure. I think I'd better read the passage one more time.

If Jesus had succumbed to the temptation, and acquired all power on earth, then everything in the world would probably be fantastic. Everyone would be happy, and no one would suffer, etc. However, we would not have free will, the choice to accept God or reject him. I think that decision is critical to God. I believe that God is so loving that he wants a true relationship with us, one that we desire too. In a relationship one partner can be as loving and caring as possible, but if the other has not made the decision to love, then it means nothing. Does that make sense?

Another one I am confused about is the following:

In the mornings, before the sun rose to high above the hilltops, I went jogging along dirt roads that coiled among the stalky stands of saguaro cacti. Wary of rattlesnakes and scorpions, I mostly kept my head down looking at the road, but one morning on a new route I glanced up to see a shimmering resort looming before me, almost like a mirage. I jogged closer and discovered two Olympic swimming pools, aerobic workout rooms, a cinder jogging trail, lush gardens, a baseball diamond, soccer fields, and horse stables. The facilities, I learned, belonged to a famous eating disorder clinic that caters to movie stars and athletes. The clinic features the latest twelve-step programme techniques, has a staff well stocked with Ph.D.s and M.D.s, and charges its clients about $300 per day.

I jogged slowly back to the jumble of houses and buildings at the Wycliffe base, keenly aware of their contrast to the gleaming architecture of the eating disorder clinic. One institution endeavoured to save souls, to prepare people to serve God here and in eternity, the other endeavoured to save bodies, to prepare people to enjoy this life. It seemed obvious which institution the world honours.

My immediate answer would be that the point is a simple illustration of how many resources we use improving the physical body, when the deeper issue – that is generally ignored – is the state of our soul (seen from a Christian perspective). I would be disappointed if Yancey, in any way, failed to appreciate the importance of human beings' right to live well (that wouldn't be very Christian either), but seen in context with the rest I think he's just considering the differences.

> 'Blessed are the unfortunate . . .' I don't quite follow that. I have read it again and again – and one place or another I lose track . . . Yet at times I feel I understand it as I am reading the words, but as soon as my eyes lift off the page, it's gone.

I think that one sounds tricky. In the Sermon on the Mount, Jesus talks about the poor in spirit . . . the point being that the less you are in yourself, the more reliant you become on God. However, 'the unfortunate' sounds rather funny. I can't remember the context either. Although, even if I could there's no guarantee that I would be able to come up with a decent answer.

> I surprise myself by making such an effort to understand all of this without, as mentioned, being dissuaded by my own inadequacies – that I make mistakes and learn through them. However, sometimes I think it's unfair how Philip Yancey writes that God's kingdom, which grows amid all evil, is described by Jesus as being wheat growing up among weeds. Difficult to explain. I just think that was a little weak of Jesus . . . as I wrote before, not only for the fact that I haven't found anything inside me to which I can attach the idea that God does exist. I am trying. But to think that I am only part of those weeds – a boring weed that nobody bothers to play with other than other weeds. I sincerely hope I am more than that in *your* eyes. I feel left out sometimes when it comes down to issues of faith, heaven, etc . . . and I am, because ultimately I have chosen to be. I don't know . . . but . . . ah . . . now I don't know what to

write any more. This has turned into the worst case of gibberish so far.

This is definitely not gibberish. I understand you completely. The description of the corn that grows up in different ways is directed at how we as people relate to the message of God. It does, however, in no way describe the way in which we view other people. Seen through Christian eyes you are just as beautiful a creation as I am, and just as valuable. In fact, if I described you as merely a useless weed I would be directly criticising a piece of God's creation. In that case it would be me that had the problem in my relationship to God. I won't deny that you could run into some Christians, with a distorted view of things, who live with the understanding that all non-Christians are looked upon with overbearing eyes. But . . . hmm . . . you can find ugly extremities in almost any circumstances.

In any case, I can guarantee you would be treated with the utmost respect if you met some of my Christian friends. If I can allow myself a moment of personal joy, then I am extremely thankful for my circle of friends. I don't know anyone who is so good at including other people and making them feel welcome. You have obviously met Jan-Erik and Mai and David. I hope you didn't feel that they regarded you as a boring thistle. ☺

Preconception number 1 has been quickly thrown aside: I didn't think Christians touched alcohol. Why/why not?

You will meet both Christians who believe alcohol is from the devil, and those who have a more liberal stance towards it. There are some good arguments for not touching it altogether – but you won't get any of them right now since Jan is coming over in a little while and we are going to eat dinner!

However, I have a very relaxed attitude towards alcohol. I seldom get really drunk, but if it does happen it's not planned. I don't really concern myself too much if I have one or two beers too many when in good company and the conversation is flowing, etc.

– – –

From: Stine Forsberg
Sent: December 04, 2002 8:19 pm
To: Mikael R. Andreasen
Subject: Re:

Hi Mikael,

Thanks for your assignment on grace. It was really good and helped me understand a few things a little better. It's strange, once again, how some of the things I had been wondering about recently suddenly found new meaning in what you had written. Not to mention the things I otherwise would have dumped on you in the last email.

I think you are gifted in explaining yourself. A lot of things come across in a manner that's simple and almost obvious.

I am on the last chapter in the book, then I'll return it. Although I could almost have fallen in love with Jesus previously, we fell out yesterday. I had forgotten how the Sermon on the Mount always made me feel so offended.

You are obviously permitted to express personal happiness. ☺ Warm and welcoming would be the first words that spring to mind after having met some of your friends. They seem very sweet. Is Mai also a Christian?

Anyway, now I am heading out in the December cold. Have a good evening.

Stine

– – –

From: Mikael R. Andreasen
Sent: December 05, 2002 0:10 am
To: Stine Forsberg
Subject: Re:

A few comments on your comments:

> Thanks for your assignment on grace. It was really good and helped me understand a few things a little better. It's strange, once again, how some of the things I had been wondering about recently suddenly found new meaning in what you had written. Not to mention the things I otherwise would have dumped on you in the last email.

Thanks! I'm glad to hear it. I find it difficult to judge how comprehensively I should express myself, especially when I am ignorant as to the extent of your prior knowledge. That said,

I am glad that what I write gives meaning – in one way or another. ☺

> I am on the last chapter in the book, then I'll return it. Although I could almost have fallen in love with Jesus previously, we fell out yesterday. I had forgotten how the Sermon on the Mount always made me feel so offended.

Hmm . . . the Sermon on the Mount?! Please elaborate.

> You are obviously permitted to express personal happiness. ☺ Warm and welcoming would be the first words that spring to mind after having met some of your friends. They seem very sweet. Is Mai also a Christian?

Yes, Mai is also a Christian.

_ _ _

From: Stine Forsberg
Sent: December 05, 2002 0:56 am
To: Mikael R. Andreasen
Subject: Re:

I'll refer to some bits from your emails:

> Thanks! I'm glad to hear it. I find it difficult to judge how comprehensively I should express myself, especially when I am ignorant as to the extent of your prior knowledge. That said, I am glad that what I write gives meaning – in one way or another. ☺

It does, as I said. On many levels. Most of all you are

good at setting things straight for me, so that I can smooth out tangled threads. That's very nice . . . or . . . it's beautiful. ☺ Thanks again...

Hmm . . . the Sermon on the Mount?! Please elaborate.

OK then . . .

I have just always thought they were some strict rules to follow. Obviously not the part about loving one another, but more about setting perfection as the ideal. That is impossible to reach. It has always surprised me that very few people seem to think that Tolstoy's way of living was wrong. He attempted to live out the rigorous rules that Jesus laid down and it ended up destroying him. I have discussed this at length with people, and yet remain unconvinced that this ideal is something that is fair to ask of us. How on earth is it possible to live our lives according to it? I assume we disagree completely on this? ☺

I read something today, his name escapes me, about how it isn't necessary to follow those rules any more. Something to do with the times having changed, and it's no longer expected that we can stringently follow them. I don't know if this man was just a nobody, or was even capable of explaining it, but I also thought it was good to be a little wary . . . It's late, and I thought I was going to bed early today. Nope – that didn't happen.

Sleep well and dream sweet dreams.

Stine

- - -

From: Mikael R. Andreasen
Sent: December 05, 2002 2:32 pm
To: Stine Forsberg
Subject: Re:

To quote your email:

OK then . . .

I have just always thought they were some strict rules to follow. Obviously not the part about loving one another, but more about setting perfection as the ideal. That is impossible to reach. It has always surprised me that very few people seem to think that Tolstoy's way of living was wrong. He attempted to live out the rigorous rules that Jesus laid down and it ended up destroying him. I have discussed this at length with people, and yet remain unconvinced that this ideal is something that is fair to ask of us. How on earth is it possible to live our lives according to it? I assume we disagree completely on this? ☺

I read something today, his name escapes me, about how it isn't necessary to follow those rules any more. Something to do with the times having changed, and it's no longer expected that we can stringently follow them. I don't know if this man was just a nobody, or was even capable of explaining it, but I also thought it was good to be a little wary . . . It's late, and I thought I was going to bed early today. Nope – that didn't happen.

Did you read Hanna's piece that I sent as an attachment with my assignment?[6]

Naturally it's impossible to live up to such demands. As Hanna rightly puts it, both God and humankind are aware of this impossibility, and yet God asks it. Why would he do that? It is simply showing people that they cannot save themselves. Therefore, we are dependent on God's grace. That is the core of Christianity. People have fallen away from God, yet God offers himself out of love to humankind, and as we accept and believe that Jesus died as a substitute for us, then the atonement between God and humankind has been made possible. Yes, it sounds completely bizarre. I sometimes think about how complicated it all is, and yet, at the same time, it's so incredibly simple (if you actually believe in it). ☺

This is where Christianity separates itself from any other beliefs. There is nothing we can do to save ourselves – except believe and receive. I think that's wild.

I don't know how much I will be able to email in the next few days. I have to go into the studio today and tomorrow to help record a song for a mini-CD we are making at our church. Would you like to borrow the other Philip Yancey book, *What's So Amazing About Grace?* On the back cover are the following fantastic words:

> There is nothing we can do to make God love us more.
> There is nothing we can do to make God love us less.

All the best, on this grey Thursday.

Mikael

– – –

From: Stine Forsberg
Sent: December 05, 2002 7:01 pm
To: Mikael R. Andreasen
Subject: Re:

I shall quote bits of your email and respond to them:

> Did you read Hanna's piece that I sent as an attachment
> with my assignment? Naturally it's impossible to live up to
> such demands. As Hanna rightly puts it, both God and
> humankind are aware of this impossibility, and yet God asks
> it. Why would he do that? It simply shows people that they
> cannot save themselves. Therefore, we are dependent on
> God's grace. That is the core of Christianity. People have
> fallen away from God, yet God offers himself out of love to
> humankind, and as we accept and believe that Jesus died as
> a substitute for us, then the atonement between God and
> humankind has been made possible. Yes, it sounds com-
> pletely bizarre. I sometimes think about how complicated it
> all is, and yet, at the same time, it's so incredibly simple
> (if you actually believe in it). ☺

> This is where Christianity separates itself from any other
> beliefs. There is nothing we can do to save ourselves – except
> believe and receive. I think that's wild.

Yes, I read the beautiful words after your assignment.
Sometimes I'm just too quick to disregard the possibility of placing myself in those things that seem so
difficult for me to understand. It's funny that the things
that I wonder about – and send over to you [as an
agent] to have clarified – I end up bumping into in a

later, more in-depth mail. When I read later what you wrote, it gives an almost clear meaning. ☺ Christianity apparently isn't as complicated as I had thought. Come to think of it, there are quite a few things that I have changed my opinion on completely in a very short space of time. It's strange when the change happens over such a short period of time, and is so apparent. Yet, no matter how much I want to believe in all this to do with God, Jesus, etc., etc. – you wrote something about daring – but it's not even the lack of courage that's holding me back . . . I just can't. At least not at the moment.

> I don't know how much I will be able to email in the next few days. I have to go into the studio today and tomorrow to help record a song for a mini-CD we are making at our church. Would you like to borrow the other Philip Yancey book, *What's So Amazing About Grace?* On the back cover are the following fantastic words:

I am also moving this weekend so my computer will be without connection to anything at all for a few days. I have no idea how I will manage. I have a bad feeling about it. ☺ Ah, I'm going to miss these exchanges, but perhaps we will soon meet face to face again, for a change. I have a book for you, and would definitely like to borrow the one on grace.

> There is nothing we can do to make God love us more.
> There is nothing we can do to make God love us less.

Wow . . . ☺

It sounds really exciting with the recording of that CD. Although I don't completely understand how – apart from attending – you are connected to 'your' church. Especially as you are about to go ahead with this project now . . . it seems far from just a Sunday visit?!?

Can you believe it, this week has flown past. As I think about how fast it's gone, I almost feel like it's accelerating, and I am about to fall off . . .

Stine

– – –

From: Mikael R. Andreasen
Sent: December 09, 2002 11:58 pm
To: Stine Forsberg
Subject: Re:

You wrote:

> Yes, I read the beautiful words after your assignment. Sometimes I'm just too quick to disregard the possibility of placing myself in those things that seem so difficult for me to understand. It's funny that the things that I wonder about – and send over to you [as an agent] to have clarified – I end up bumping into in a later, more in-depth mail. When I read later what you wrote, it gives an almost clear meaning. ☺ Christianity apparently isn't as complicated as I had thought. Come to think of it, there are quite a few things that I have changed my opinion on completely in a very short space of time. It's strange when the change happens over such a

short period of time, and is so apparent. Yet, no matter how much I want to believe in all this to do with God, Jesus, etc., etc. – you wrote something about daring – but it's not even the lack of courage that's holding me back . . . I just can't. At least not at the moment.

And that is completely fine. I hope you can feel relaxed about all this. Heaven forbid that you walk around and go crazy from it all. Perhaps one day you will feel you are ready to believe, and perhaps not. You will find that out for yourself. However, if God is interested in being your friend, then I think it's only fair that you ask him to reveal himself in one way or another. I think it's totally fair to present God with tests. To reveal himself to you, if he really is there. The most important thing is that you are ready for it, not to rush anything. And yes, you are still just as nice regardless of whether you believe or not. I have told you that before.

. . . but perhaps we will soon meet face to face again, for a change. I have a book for you, and would definitely like to borrow the one on grace.

Hmm, when is a convenient time to meet up? Maybe the 18th or 19th? I am busy the next few days. I have actually been busy the past few days too, but the 18th or 19th would suit me fine.

It sounds really exciting with the recording of that CD. Although I don't completely understand how – apart from attending – you are connected to 'your' church. Especially as you are about to go ahead with this project now . . . it seems far from just a Sunday visit?!?

We managed to record a song for a three-track CD we are giving out at church. The song we recorded turned out to be almost nine minutes long. The lyrics are as follows, and written by our priest (inspired by Kierkegaard):

When all has become silent
and my soul has found its rest
when I dare to open my inner
and receive the life you gave.
I become no one else
but myself
– and am one with you.
Then the heavens part
you are the highest power
I become no one else
But one with you.

It turned out to be a great song and from February anyone who visits our church can get a free CD. For my part, at the moment it's 'only' Sunday visits. During the week there are smaller groups from the church who meet at each other's houses and eat and have a relaxed time together. The church I go to is called Copenhagen Vineyard (the same church that the guys from Glorybox and Jan-Erik and Mai go to). It's a great church to attend.

- - -

From: Stine Forsberg
Sent: December 10, 2002 7:09 am
To: Mikael R. Andreasen
Subject: Re:

Hi Mikael,

I hope you've had a really, really good weekend. I can imagine it's been busy. Doesn't recording and all that usually take longer than expected? I have been moving and moving and moving . . . and even though it's been hard – since I am not the strongest creature on earth – it's been nice. Now I'm just looking forward to putting everything in its place.

I cannot even think about Christmas until my bed has been moved into the position that makes it seem comfiest, and all my books and CDs are up on the shelves and out of the huge moving boxes.

Did you notice it snowed yesterday? I was travelling home and I got hit by lots of flakes that – to my great consternation – neither settled on the ground nor floated around for longer. For a moment there, I closed my eyes and imagined I was in Norway where the snow falling from the sky actually settled on the ground . . . on top of the freshly fallen metre and a half or so . . . I was quite disappointed to open my eyes and find myself cycling on Nørrebrogade in cold, snow-less Copenhagen. Speaking about the weather, I hope you have bought yourself a good winter coat . . . it is cold outside. My hands are already going red and freezing at the thought that I have to be outside in less than an hour. In a moment I will take a long bath so that I can get warm before-hand.

The 18th and the 19th work perfectly for me. I am really busy this week at school since it's 'feature week' and they have split all the students up and are taking them out to see different workplaces. It's good fun. The woman I am working with thinks it's fun if we stay at school almost the whole week, and just prepare . . . so I almost never go home – but that's fine. At the weekend I have promised to visit my little brother and take him to Århus to visit Rikke. It's bad timing – in that I have to go home next weekend anyway – but it doesn't matter. I am going home to my mother (I must live in some sort of dysfunctional family in your eyes . . . parents divorced, my father + lover, and now another kid on the way, to mention a few of the intricacies).

It would be great to meet up, and logical, since I have almost a whole box full of things I have to give to you. To tell you the truth, I have also bought something for you. Don't think of it as an official Christmas present. It's a mixture of that and something else I haven't quite figured out. It just seemed fitting, as one day I was just starting to think about presents and I realised that I wanted to give you something. And since it would be impossible for me to give you back anything spiritual, I thought you would have to settle for something materialistic instead. ☺

Hope you enjoy yourself until we meet up! And have a good day at work!

All the best,

Stine

‒ ‒ ‒

From: Mikael R. Andreasen
Sent: December 10, 2002 7:18 am
To: Stine Forsberg
Subject: Re:

I think the 19th suits me best.

‒ ‒ ‒

From: Stine Forsberg
Sent: December 10, 2002 7:21 am
To: Mikael R. Andreasen
Subject: Re:

The 19th it is then!

– – –

From: Mikael R. Andreasen
Sent: December 10, 2002 9:18 pm
To: Stine Forsberg
Subject: Re:

Ahhh, I just get so upset when I read the comments from M. C. Kristen on Svingninger.[7] It's such a tiring manner in which to express your faith. However, as in all circles of society, there are a few tiring people lurking among the Christians too. Hmm, I think I'll call Jan-Erik and see if he wants to head down to Mc Kluud for an evening beer.

I should go to bed, but can't be bothered.

Bye,

Mikael

– – –

From: Stine Forsberg
Sent: December 10, 2002 9:27 pm
To: Mikael R. Andreasen
Subject: Re:

Yeah, that's a shame. Just as I am getting close to understanding all of this, and seeing that there doesn't need to be this huge difference between us, then I run into these pathetic pieces from M. C. Kristen, and all of it seems confusing again. I guess it's easy for you to see how these preconceptions arise?!? Nice that you are having an evening beer – I think I'll settle for milk. I completely forgot that buttermilk exists, and now I am craving it . . . all the time.

Stine

- - -

From: Mikael R. Andreasen
Sent: December 10, 2002 9:53 pm
To: Stine Forsberg
Subject: Re:

I decided against going to Mc Kluud. I was, after all, too tired.

What irritates me the most about M. C. Kristen is that he just spews out words without being able to enter into a conversation, to explain, to listen, to . . . They are just words people cannot relate to. That irritates me, but these people exist.

How about making mulled wine here, on the 19th?

– mik –

- - -

From: Stine Forsberg
Sent: December 10, 2002 10:09 pm
To: Mikael R. Andreasen
Subject: Re:

Wine sounds fun . . . good idea.

You're right; understanding doesn't come from a one-sided river of words, but from discussions and ordinary conversations. It's good that you were there to say something, otherwise I would have just shaken my head at all of you. ☺

– – –

From: Mikael R. Andreasen
Sent: December 10, 2002 10:36 pm
To: Stine Forsberg
Subject: Re:

Previously you wrote something about how I must think you come from a dysfunctional family. I think there were elements of irony in what you wrote, but no, I don't at all. I don't think that way about non-Christians. That they have terrible lives because they are divorced, have a lover, or whatever. Their outlook is completely different to mine, and therefore a different set of rules, ideals and agreements apply. If I weren't a Christian, I myself would probably have lived such an – in your own words – unhappy life. Ah, I really think I'm jumbling my words now.

In any case, there's no form of overbearing or con-descending attitude from my side towards people who choose to live their lives differently from the way I do. Even though I believe that truth exists, it's not hard for me to understand and respect other people's way of life – no matter how obscure they may be (not that your family is obscure ☺). I think you understand what I'm trying to say. In short, that I have the greatest respect for other people and their way of interpreting the world and living in it.

– mik –

‒ ‒ ‒

From: Stine Forsberg
Sent: December 10, 2002 10:42 pm
To: Mikael R. Andreasen
Subject: Re:

Who has made you so sweet?!?

Now I'm off to bed, to try and sleep through the night without waking up . . .

Stine

The comments were – as you mentioned – for fun. I think by now I have seen the way in which you relate to other people who don't live their lives in the way you do, and I think that's great!

‒ ‒ ‒

From: Stine Forsberg
Sent: December 12, 2002 0:29 am
To: Mikael R. Andreasen
Subject: Re:

Such is the extent that Philip Yancey fascinates me . . . I think I'll skip my sleep and read instead . . .

– – –

From: Mikael R. Andreasen
Sent: December 12, 2002 0:34 am
To: Stine Forsberg
Subject: Re:

No, you need to get your sleep. ☺

Yeah, I probably do too. I just ended up writing a long submission to Svingninger. Hmm, I'm not really that happy with it. However, I couldn't just keep quiet. It was in response to all that confusion with M. C. Kristen. I really don't want to appear as an argumentative person, and wouldn't have, except a few recent comments by him caused me to respond. I'll probably get told off now . . .

Now, I'm off to bed.

Ciao,

Mikael

– – –

From: Stine Forsberg
Sent: December 12, 2002 0:43 am
To: Mikael R. Andreasen
Subject: Re:

I know how important sleep is. I will just read to the next big point, and then close my eyes. I will also read your response soon. It will be fun to see how I would look upon it if I didn't know who you were . . .

Stine

— — —

From: Stine Forsberg
Sent: December 12, 2002 9:17 pm
To: Mikael R. Andreasen
Subject: Re:

Ouch – I have packed your present, and the stuff I was wrapping it in was incredibly painful to make. I have pricked myself with a needle a thousand times and have now got lots of cuts on my fingertips. The real reason being there wasn't enough light . . . so I couldn't see properly . . .

I'm going to sleep soon (well, I say I will, but in reality will probably be up all night), because I do, after all, have to go to Jutland tomorrow, and didn't get much sleep last night. Before I head off I just wanted to say that I liked the response you wrote on the website. How it will be viewed by people who have never met you, I can't say. Some people will most probably jump to conclusions and think you are the same as M.C. Kristen. I think you made a fine attempt of moving away from his sharp manner of expressing his views. Once again, you formulate yourself so well . . . I assume you've come out top in many discussions in your life.

I don't know how it affects you knowing that so many people say so many negative things about 'that group' of Christians, who they think are all the same (which is in itself unjustified), and I can only truly associate with the hordes of people who find it hard to understand the whole thing, but I think I can also understand now how others can gradually – at least to some extent – turn their resistance – created by great ignorance – to the highest respect. This is probably due to how I am receiving such high respect for my, and other non-Christians', way of living. It is weird though – I see the same things that everyone else reads on the Svingninger forum, and yet find myself sympathising most with your responses . . . no . . . I need not go to bed. I have decided. I am about to divulge things that make me confused when it comes to Christianity . . . and that God guy. ☺

– – –

From: Mikael R. Andreasen
Sent: December 20, 2002 0:36 am
To: Stine Forsberg
Subject: Re:

. . . and a short while ago I sat here listening to a Damien Jurado concert and opening my present from you. I don't know if it was the smartest way to get the pearl chain off the box, but with the slightest touch the whole thing broke and my bed was covered in pearls. I had to laugh. Thanks so much for the lovely card. In the same way, you too have become a great new acquaintance. It's been so enriching to have these email conversations with you – for my sake they can continue a bit longer! ☺

Thank you so much for the present. I like it very much. I glanced quickly through the books and look forward to a chance to sit down quietly and enjoy them. But – with all this talk of Christmas presents – I cannot help but feel that you have spent too much money on mine. However, I won't think about that right now, instead I'll just be grateful – 'also today there is reason to be thankful' – so thanks!

I didn't manage to ask you what you thought of the video I showed you of us playing in church. I would be interested to know if you thought it was weird, if you were surprised a church could look like that, or . . . ? Tiredness is slowly creeping up on me, and despite plans to stay up and play with my guitar I think I will just fall asleep.

Enjoy Christmas with your family and hide yourself away on New Year's Eve.[8]

Adieu,

Mikael

– – –

From: Stine Forsberg
Sent: December 21, 2002 11:33 am
To: Mikael R. Andreasen
Subject: Re:

Hi Mikael,

As I've said before, you are a really great friend. There was apparently no smart way of removing the pearls – I ended up ruining it myself the first time around. Suddenly there were pearls everywhere. I hope you noticed how the pearls were not placed randomly, but there was a system behind it. ☺

I'm heading out to buy one last present, then it's back home to cook a good dinner and watch a nice film . . . perhaps *Platoon* – since I haven't seen it yet in my new surroundings . . . funny if it makes for a significant new experience...

If you are bored you're more than welcome to stop over, I can guarantee you there's an abundance of food and war films . . .

In regards to the video I watched at your place, it was very interesting. I'm very glad I got to see it. Thanks. The music itself was beautiful – regardless of whether or not I can relate to the message. I was just letting it all sink in, which is why I didn't fire off a response immediately. It was interesting to see how a service could run away like that. That was a positive surprise. It was, however, quite difficult to relate to some of the reactions from the church-goers. Some of them gave themselves over completely, and that was difficult for me to comprehend. It seemed a little overwhelming, if I have to be honest. The rest of the thoughts will follow later.

Bye,

Stine

– – –

From: Stine Forsberg
Sent: December 29, 2002 12:55 pm
To: Mikael R. Andreasen
Subject: Re:

Hey Mikael,

Thank you so much for lending me the book.[9] I almost couldn't go to bed last night because I allowed myself a small peek when I came home, and it was already late. So I was left hanging. I'm not too pleased to be the first one that bends the pages on your new book – you should have done that. However, the book is good. It follows on with similar ideas and examples as the first book I read by him, but he explains things clearly and touches on the subjects so well – *so* well.

Have a good trip to church today. Say hello to people for me.

Stine

- - -

From: Mikael R. Andreasen
Sent: December 30, 2002 4:20 am
To: Stine Forsberg
Subject: Re:

Hi there!

I have just got home. Should have been in bed hours ago. Hmm.

I'm glad the book is to your taste – I'm looking forward to reading it myself. I received your greeting on Svingninger! Thanks. I will get around to replying, but the days pass with this and that, and of course preparations for New Year, so it will have to wait a bit.

Now, goodnight.

– mik –

- - -

From: Stine Forsberg
Sent: December 30, 2002 9:07 am
To: Mikael R. Andreasen
Subject: Re:

I was so far away, dreaming, when the alarm clock started ringing. After a week off it's difficult to remember what it feels like to go to work. My dreams were so beautiful that it's almost a shame I had to get up . . .

I reread what I sent you on Svingninger and you don't have to reply to it. It seemed a bit much when I read it through again. What I'm contemplating most, at the moment, is whether or not you ever feel deserted by God. So, when you have the time . . .

I read, coincidentally, a part of the book that speaks about an angel: that to be able to carry out the will of Daniel's prayer, received strength from a power named Mikael . . . you are a man of many talents. ☺

Have a good day.

Stine

– – –

From: Mikael R. Andreasen
Sent: January 12, 2003 12:45 pm
To: Stine Forsberg
Subject: Re:

Hi!

So far it's been a good weekend. I hope yours has been even better. ☺

Come to think of it, on Saturday we are holding an event at our church called Winterlight. It's a whole day set aside for stillness and letting go. The programme will include some music, some teaching on prayer and meditation, then communion and, after that, a few hours' silence. Afterwards Solrun, Jan-Erik, Sarah and I will play an hour or so of mellow music. We will be doing some tracks from our Christmas EP. I don't know exactly what Sarah will be playing, but usually any time she plays acoustic guitar it's fantastic.

Anyway, I was just wondering if you were interested in dropping by – if so, you're most welcome. Even if you want to come just for the music, that's fine. The entrance fee is 30Kr, to cover expenses, etc. If you don't feel like it, then that's cool too!

All for now,

– mik –

‒ ‒ ‒

From: Stine Forsberg
Sent: January 12, 2003 2:50 pm
To: Mikael R. Andreasen
Subject: Re:

Thanks for the invitation! I've suddenly got an upset stomach . . . from indecision! Even though I think it could be interesting, I'm a little afraid that I would feel out of place just turning up on my own. Not many outsiders just turn up, do they?

Can I be allowed to come just for the music, even though I would like to stay the whole time?

Hmm . . . maybe I should just convince myself to come for the whole thing . . .

We are going to make food and eat out at school on Saturday. I'm not sure what time of day that is, but it's probably in the afternoon.

Have a wonderful Sunday.

Stine

– – –

From: Mikael R. Andreasen
Sent: January 12, 2003 6:05 pm
To: Stine Forsberg
Subject: Re:

I apologise for giving you an upset stomach! ☺

Feel free to come exactly when you want to – and also just to see us play. We will start playing at around 5:30 pm, maybe a bit before. It's a relatively open programme. The idea behind the day is just to take some time to relax and be silent. The majority of those coming will be relaxing with God, but if you want to bring a book, that's absolutely fine. It's also OK if you don't come . . . although I can't see it being too dangerous. ☺

Adieu,

– mik –

From: Stine Forsberg
Sent: January 12, 2003 8:17 pm
To: Mikael R. Andreasen
Subject: Re:

Don't worry about my stomach. That's my concern.

Think, think, think . . . I would at least like to see you guys play.

Stine

From: Stine Forsberg
Sent: January 13, 2003 0:14 am
To: Mikael R. Andreasen
Subject: Re:

I was out at Nicholas's and Stine's house. We chatted and ate sweets. I have just got home now, completely soaked. Ugh!

I hope I have caught you before you've gone to bed. I couldn't bear the thought of the last thing on your mind being how strange it is that Stine doesn't just come on Saturday. I know you said the thing about it not being dangerous for fun, but let me explain . . . I would really love to come, and I wish I were braver, but there are just a few things I need to clear up with God before I can. So don't think it's because I don't care, but I think I'll just settle for coming when you guys play. Another time . . . I sincerely hope that's OK.

Goodnight,

Stine

— — —

From: Mikael R. Andreasen
Sent: January 13, 2003 0:35 am
To: Stine Forsberg
Subject: Re:

Hi!

Tobias has just left. You're soaked? Has it been raining? Hmm . . .

No, I don't think it's strange that you find it hard to make your mind up. I can completely understand your hesitation. I will simply feel grateful if you come while we are playing. That you even make the effort is nice.

However, it's so important for me to point out that you don't have to have everything in order with God before you enter a church. Church is not for perfect people. A church (ideally) should be a place where you can come, as weak as you may be, and find safety. It's important for me that you really understand that you can come exactly as you are. With all your beliefs, or lack thereof. Also, that you won't be attacked with this and that, and asked a million questions. Now, I don't want it to seem like I'm trying to convince you

– I'm not – I just want you to get an idea of what a church really is like.

I can't understand why I have been going around lately feeling ill. It might be down to stress-symptoms. It's as though I can never completely shake off this cold, not to mention my problems in sleeping. Ha, funny how there's three S's in a row in stress-symptoms. Now I'm off to brush my teeth, crawl into bed, and hope that sleep embraces me immediately.

– mik –

– – –

From: Stine Forsberg
Sent: January 13, 2003 0:49 am
To: Mikael R. Andreasen
Subject: Re:

It' been raining like crazy. Funny how you failed to notice it, although rain is not as noticeable as snow – you don't see it as clearly when you look out of the window. I know that you don't have to be perfect to enter a church, but there's just something that tells me it's not the right time. Even when I think about it clearly, there's still something that tells me that I shouldn't . . . so unless I can convince myself otherwise, I will turn up later. I know – it's so cowardly.

I'm sorry that you feel unwell.

Thanks for the CDs. I just listened to the cover album by Slowdive. I really like the Slowdive album: *Souvlaki*. Anyway, I'm gonna put the other CD on. I can't wait to hear it. Where will I find the time for sleep?

Stine

– – –

From: Mikael R. Andreasen
Sent: January 13, 2003 0:55 am
To: Stine Forsberg
Subject: Re:

Stop all this talk of cowardice. ☺

It's totally understandable that you are hesitant, there's nothing cowardly about that. Feel free to tell me what it is you feel you need to clear up with God. It sounds interesting but, again, don't feel you have to tell me any more than you want. Now, I'm off to bed (and this time I mean it!).

See you . . .

Mikael

– – –

From: Stine Forsberg
Sent: January 13, 2003 6:12 pm
To: Mikael R. Andreasen
Subject: Re:

Hi Mikael,

Cowardice, I have to admit I still lean towards it even
though you tell me I shouldn't.

Hmm . . . it's as though God has caught me by surprise.
All those things I couldn't understand before have
slowly, before my own eyes, become something I can
grasp. Still, I hesitate because everything has happened
so quickly, and is still a little strange. What's strange is
that I feel this way, and yet don't think it strange. Does
that make sense? I think it's weird how I suddenly care
about it, and even search for it . . . and I've already
written that a thousand times before. ☺

One thing I feel the need to clear up is how my
motives of late will suddenly look, and decide if all of
this is right or not. 'One thing or other' (which personi-
fies me – the little coward, I believe) tells me to wait
for a while because I am not quite sure how to react
to certain things. Deep down I feel it could be a good
idea, but that 'something or other' inside me disagrees.
I don't think I would be able to just come along and
treat it as something you believe because I would end
up involving myself too much in my thoughts and
other things far too much. And right now that seems a
little overwhelming. Unfortunately (a coward, I

believe . . . ☺) I doubt that has helped you one bit in understanding what I meant?

Bye,

Stine

_ _ _

From: Mikael R. Andreasen
Sent: January 13, 2003 21:36 pm
To: Stine Forsberg
Subject: Re: Re:

It seems that every time I write an email to you I have to convince you that I understand what you're writing. However, it's not just a standard answer, or meant to suggest I'm writing on auto-response.

Regardless of how chaotic your last email might have been, I really think you expressed some things that made a lot of sense. Once again, I think it's fascinating to be allowed – from a distance – to follow what goes on in someone else's head – no matter what it leads to.

Tra la la,

Mikael

– – –

From: Stine Forsberg
Sent: January 14, 2003 2:26 am
To: Mikael R. Andreasen
Subject: Re:

Yet again I thought I would go to bed early. Ann Kristin's birthday party dragged on longer than expected, passed with lots of mindless banter, and once again I have just come in the door . . .

I can't quite escape it myself, as you can understand, and end up contradicting myself and inventing new things and theories to constantly have opinions on. What exactly is it you think made sense in that last portion of gibberish I sent you? (I'm at a loss myself, so please enlighten me . . .). I have decided to drop the censor on my emails and can't be bothered to read them through before I send them. There is no point in trying to make chaos sound pretty and balanced. ☺ I hope that's OK! So from now on the thoughts are coming directly from my heart, or wherever it is they come from. Bear with me . . .

Now, I feel I need some sleep. The clock is ticking towards six, which means that there are only four hours before my alarm clock goes off, and I will set it half an hour later – after which I will set it forward another half-hour. Then at precisely seven I will get up, and be in a real rush. Life is beautiful . . . and right now I just wish I could sleep for ever!

I hope you have fallen asleep already and are having some sweet dreams.

Stine

– – –

From: Mikael R. Andreasen
Sent: January 14, 2003 10:15 pm
To: Stine Forsberg
Subject: Re:

Hi!

I'm counting on going to bed early tonight.

I think it makes a lot of sense when you write about wanting to understand your motives – in other words, that you don't, simply because you have read four books about God and have perhaps been lulled into a notion that God exists, suddenly agree with this and that. I think it's healthy to sit down and really think things through, and even challenge God to make himself known to you.

It turned out to be really easy for me to read the email you described as gibberish. It's as though the words flowed well, like a stream of stringent, logical consciousness.

Now, my eyes won't stay open for any longer.

Bye,

Mikael

– – –
From: Stine Forsberg
Sent: January 14, 2003 10:25 pm
To: Mikael R. Andreasen
Subject: Re:

I'll have to skip my evening shower – it wakes me up too much. All I need right now is sleep . . . tomorrow is going to be a long day, and Thursday's going to be a long day, and Friday's going to be a long day, and Saturday's going to be a long day . . . gosh. Therefore, tonight I shall sleep deeply and long.

You wrote:

> I think it makes a lot of sense when you write about wanting to understand your motives – in other words, that you don't, simply because you have read four books about God and have perhaps been lulled into a notion that God exists, suddenly agree with this and that. I think it's healthy to sit down and really think things through, and even challenge God to make himself known to you.

I agree, I think. ☺

Sleep well.

– – –

From: Stine Forsberg
Sent: January 14, 2003 10:45 pm
To: Mikael R. Andreasen
Subject: Re:

An addition, even though I am actually far away in a deep sleep . . .

I just started to think that it's not only down to the four books I have read. ☺ Otherwise, agreed!

– – –

From: Mikael R. Andreasen
Sent: January 14, 2003 11:03 pm
To: Stine Forsberg
Subject: Re:

'I just started to think that it's not only down to the four books I have read. ☺ '

Please elaborate. ☺

Now, to bed!

– mik –

– – –

From: Stine Forsberg
Sent: January 15, 2003 8:08 am
To: Mikael R. Andreasen
Subject: Re:

'Please elaborate. ☺'

Hmm . . . that's gonna take time, and courage, but I will . . .

Have a good day at work.

Stine

– – –

From: Stine Forsberg
Sent: January 19, 2003 4:53 am
To: Mikael R. Andreasen
Subject: Re:

I truly hope you've had a great day! Thank you so much for letting me come to see you guys play. It was both a lovely and a peculiar experience . . . I'll admit to, yet again, having been impressed by the music (even though it didn't always run as planned).

All that's good.

Stine

- - -

From: Mikael R. Andreasen
Sent: January 19, 2003 10:52 am
To: Stine Forsberg
Subject: Re:

Good morning.

Thank you for coming yesterday. Ha ha, I'm sorry that we were so unlucky with the sound (and not too well prepared), but yeah, I'm not going to spend too much time being irritated about it. I don't think any of us could have imagined that we wouldn't have been able to hear the backing-track in our monitors, but we couldn't. ☺ I hope you enjoyed Sarah's songs. The sound was sorted out a little later on in the evening.

What was it that made it a peculiar experience being there?

Bye bye, and have a good last day of the weekend.

Mikael

- - -

From: Stine Forsberg
Sent: January 19, 2003 4:19 pm
To: Mikael R. Andreasen
Subject: Re:

Peculiar . . . hmm, I thought for a while to find a word that fitted with what I was thinking – 'peculiar' isn't quite right. It was just strange because it stood in such contrast to what I am used to. It's good to be challenged, not in connection with the church or with you guys, but more in relation to myself. It was just something out of the ordinary and quite unexpected. In that sense it was peculiar. Peculiar, but also in a positive way.

Speaking of Sarah, I thought she was really fantastic. Had she written all the songs herself? You guys were also really good. I actually sat there hoping you would play that song you recorded and played for me, the one I liked so much. Even without that song, it was still beautiful. ☺

Did you also go to church today?

Either way, I hope you have a good Sunday. One of the best of its kind.

Stine

— — —

From: Mikael R. Andreasen
Sent: January 19, 2003 8:34 pm
To: Stine Forsberg
Subject: Re:

Hi there,

Yeah, I think Sarah wrote all the songs herself, except the one Jan and Hanna played along with. That was apparently a traditional American hymn.

Yeah, I went to church today, but left early. I sat there nodding off, due to my lack of sleep, so I thought it best just to cycle home.

I reread an old message I received from you on Svingninger. It's the one where you ask me if God ever disappoints me. I'll have to answer that one day. I have the feeling there's something else that I have forgotten to answer. I'll have to see if I can find it.

I think it's funny how you felt it was challenging to be there yesterday. It was, after all, only a few videos and some music. However, the fact that it took place inside a church made it a challenge. ☺

That's it for now.

Goodnight,

– mik –

– – –

From: Stine Forsberg
Sent: January 19, 2003 9:15 pm
To: Mikael R. Andreasen
Subject: Re:

Hi Mikael,

It's funny how you mentioned the 'challenge'. I thought to myself – and wrote it down – how strange it was that I felt that way, mainly because of the surroundings. However, I think I was taking everything into consideration – a summing-up of all the thoughts I've had in recent days. Or something like that. I don't know. What happened yesterday was just part of a huge thing that seems to be challenging me.

Does Solrun only sing when she performs with you guys? She has an amazing voice.

Stine

- - -

From: Mikael R. Andreasen
Sent: January 19, 2003 9:20 pm
To: Stine Forsberg
Subject: Re:

Yes, Solrun only sings with us at the moment. She and Jan-Erik were going to start a sort of brother/sister collaboration which is apparently going to be a little more serious than our informal gatherings. Yeah, she definitely has a gorgeous voice. I shall pass on the compliment. ☺

– – –

From: Stine Forsberg
Sent: February 13 2003, 0:02 am
To: Mikael R. Andreasen
Subject: Re:

Hi there!

I was just sitting, skimming through a book, and will now go to sleep thinking about the following words:

> And though I have the gift of prophecy,
> and understand all mysteries
> and all knowledge
> and though I have all faith
> so that I could remove mountains
> but have not love
> I am nothing.

Wow . . .

— — —

From: Mikael R. Andreasen
Sent: February 13, 2003 0:43 am
To: Stine Forsberg
Subject: Re:

I'll send you some more words from the same book. These are words that I have thought a lot about in the last year. They are:

> Do not withhold good from those to whom it is due, when it is in the power of your hand to do to. Do not say to your neighbor, 'Go, and come back, tomorrow I will give it,' when you have it with you. Do not devise evil against your neighbour, for he dwells by you for safety's sake.

The last words are especially fascinating to me: 'for he dwells by you for safety's sake'. Think if that could be a reality. That others didn't fear anything evil when spending time with you. That we could just rest in being safe. That would be insane.

— — —

From: Stine Forsberg
Sent: February 13, 2003 1:08 am
To: Mikael R. Andreasen
Subject: Re:

Wow, the words you wrote back were even more

beautiful. It's good that we have words with which to express our thoughtlife. ☺ Some people make them extremely beautiful. Is there any specific reason why you've thought about these words the past year?

I'm trying not to be too nosy. ☺

Ciao.

– – –

From: Mikael R. Andreasen
Sent: February 13, 2003 9:12 am
To: Stine Forsberg
Subject: Re:

I don't think there's any specific reason why I have thought about those words for the past few years. I just happened to notice them about a year ago and became quite fascinated by them.

[On 9 March, Stine attended Copenhagen Vineyard for the first time.]

- - -

From: Stine Forsberg
Sent: March 09, 2003 6:30 pm
To: Mikael R. Andreasen
Subject: Re:

Hi, thank you so much for today!

It was a really good experience, I think. I almost feel like going back again. ☺ However, I hope I made it clear how I feel - that I still fail to be personally convinced. I guess I just haven't felt anything substantial. In myself – because I can definitely see that you have it.

This is nonsense, I know.

Stine

– – –

From: Mikael R. Andreasen
Sent: March 09, 2003 7:22 pm
To: Stine Forsberg
Subject: Re:

Thanks to you too. ☺

I am glad that it wasn't a scary experience for you.

Flemming (the pastor) asked me what you had thought about it. I told him I thought you had found it nice enough, but had also felt a bit strange in the fact that you couldn't feel what it was all of us others thought was normal. He understood that completely – and said with a smile that you will just have to come back another time. He ended by saying that you had seemed very sweet, and that I was welcome to pass the compliment on if I thought it appropriate.

But yeah, you are welcome to come as often as you like, even 'just' as a spectator. ☺

All that's good, and a good evening.

Mikael

- - -

From: Stine Forsberg
Sent: March 09, 2003 7:59 pm
To: Mikael R. Andreasen
Subject: Re:

How did Flemming know I was only a spectator? Do I look the type? ☺

I also thought he seemed sweet. ☺ Like someone who was very kind and down-to-earth. Funny, I just thought of the words' literal meaning again. Down-to-earth . . . exactly the right word for this situation.

Yeah, it's strange, something that you don't quite know how to proceed with. Or if you're even ready for it, or want it. As I was cycling there today, I had a weird feeling in my stomach about going. Because in one way or another, I was afraid that it all might be true - perhaps even for me. And scared because even in that, there is a form of acknowledgement. I couldn't help but laugh just now when I thought of how you must laugh when thinking back on the earlier emails I sent you. How a person can change in a short, short time. ☺

Anne Mette and Andreas have just left for the cinema. Before they left we had a chance to discuss a little about church and faith. They told me, that if I found it appropriate, I could tell you that they were glad that you have inspired me and made me happy because they, even further out on the sidelines, had also changed some of their understanding of some things relating to all of this. And they thought that was nice.

Anne Mette said she thought I seemed happier, and Andreas – as far as I understood – said that the only thing he didn't get about you was that you didn't put butter and cinnamon on your rice porridge. ☺

‒ ‒ ‒

From: Mikael R. Andreasen
Sent: March 09, 2003 9:22 pm
To: Stine Forsberg
Subject: Re:

I had only told Flemming that I had a friend coming along who wasn't used to going to church. So no, it wasn't because you stuck out like a sore thumb. I would love to write a little more in response to the things you have written, but I simply have to sort out some things for school tomorrow.

However, I do put butter in my rice porridge! But no, not cinnamon. ☺

Sleep well,

Mikael

- - -

From: Mikael R. Andreasen
Sent: March 10, 2003 11:04 pm
To: Stine Forsberg
Subject: Re:

I have a sermon on a CD that Flemming gave in February which I am thinking of copying for you. It's about relationships and how the church should be a fellowship. However, only if you are interested.

- - -

From: Stine Forsberg
Sent: March 10, 2003 11:13 pm
To: Mikael R. Andreasen
Subject: Re:

I would definitely like to hear that sermon. Thank you for thinking of me.

- - -

From: Stine Forsberg
Sent: March 11, 2003 8:56 pm
To: Mikael R. Andreasen
Subject: Re:

On the subject of a birthday and a present, are you home tomorrow after 10 pm?

___

From: Mikael R. Andreasen
Sent: March 11, 2003 9:13 pm
To: Stine Forsberg
Subject: Re:

I have invited some people down to Guldregn tomorrow at 8 pm. If you want, you can drop by. It's at the beginning of Oehlenschlaegersgade, up by Vesterbrogade. It's almost directly across from the 7–11.

___

From: Stine Forsberg
Sent: March 11, 2003 9:25 pm
To: Mikael R. Andreasen
Subject: Re:

Otherwise I can come over and drop them off another day. I mean, it is on your birthday and everything.

___

From: Mikael R. Andreasen
Sent: March 11, 2003 9:34 pm
To: Stine Forsberg
Subject: Re:

It's nothing big or official. Only a few of my close friends dropping by to drink some beers, so feel free to come.

– – –

From: Stine Forsberg
Sent: March 12, 2003 6:55 am
To: Mikael R. Andreasen
Subject: Happy Birthday!

Happy birthday! I hope you have a great day. Perhaps I will drop by later so you can get your present.

Hurrah! And congratulations.

Stine

– – –

From: Mikael R. Andreasen
Sent: March 13, 2003 0.36 am
To: Stine Forsberg
Subject: Re: Happy Birthday!

Hi there,

I hope you found it enjoyable, even though you didn't know people very well – that can come with time. ☺

I have just put the Cat Power LP on. Thank you so much for the present. It was too much, but very well chosen. I hope you sleep all right tonight and feel fresh tomorrow. I just want to enjoy the fact that it's the weekend.

Goodnight,

Mikael

From: Stine Forsberg
Sent: March 13, 2003 0:47 am
To: Mikael R. Andreasen
Subject: Re: Happy Birthday!

Thank you. It was really nice. I am almost crazy about your friends. ☺ They seem so incredibly sweet and welcoming . . . I hope you have had a good day. I am very glad that you liked the presents. No, they were not too much! Perhaps well chosen, but also well deserved!

I don't think I'll get much sleep. That was the plan at least, but I am tempted to listen to the sermon. I need to hear it before I go to bed.

Love,

Stine

From: Mikael R. Andreasen
Sent: March 13, 2003 1:03 am
To: Stine Forsberg
Subject: Re: Happy Birthday!

I am glad that you like the people I love to be surrounded by. I admit to hoping a little that you could become good friends with, for example, Hanna. She is so fantastic. Add to that she loves words – which I presume you do too.

No, now I am really going to bed. The Cat Power album is on side B. It's an amazing record, and I should listen to it all the way through.

But my eyes are closing – I will have to wait till tomorrow to listen to the rest of the record. Goodnight. I hope the sermon gives you meaning on some level.

– mik –

– – –

From: Stine Forsberg
Sent: March 13, 2003 1:09 am
To: Mikael R. Andreasen
Subject: Re: Happy Birthday!

Yes, the sermon is very good. I think that despite my sleepiness I can find connections between the sermon and my parents' divorce. It just hit me. He is right. In many ways. I think I'll turn my life around. ☺

Sleep well, you 28-year-old . . .

Best wishes,

Stine

[In the following period, Stine began attending Copenhagen Vineyard regularly.]

– – –

From: Stine Forsberg
Sent: March 30, 2003 9.13 pm
To: Mikael R. Andreasen
Subject: Re:

Thanks for today. I am quite blown away by the number of nice smiles and handshakes. The people are so sweet. If I always went there, and believed in God, I think I would look forward to every Sunday . . .

Do I need to repeat myself in saying your friends are so sweet? You are blessed to have them, and vice versa.

– – –

From: Mikael R. Andreasen
Sent: March 30, 2003 10:36 pm
To: Stine Forsberg
Subject: Re:

I am happy that you want to frequent my church. And yeah, that about knowing God and going there every week is decidedly up to you. ☺

But yeah, I do look forward to it, every time I go there. It's great.

I also think my friends like you. At least, that's the impression they give me.

– – –

From: Stine Forsberg
Sent: April 06, 2003 12:26 pm
To: Mikael R. Andreasen
Subject: Re:

Hmm, would it be OK if I come to church today? I can't quite make my mind up, but I would really like to. I am also a little bit sleepy.

It could be that you've already left . . .

Stine

- - -

From: Mikael R. Andreasen
Sent: April 06, 2003 12:30 pm
To: Stine Forsberg
Subject: Re:

I haven't left quite yet, just about to have a shower and then I'm out the door. Feel free to come if you decide to. I probably don't have too much time to talk today since I'll be playing and helping pack up afterwards. But, yeah, you happen to know a few people there now. ☺

Maybe I'll see you.

– mik –

- - -

From: Stine Forsberg
Sent: April 06, 2003 12.50 pm
To: Mikael R. Andreasen
Subject: Re:

In fact it was mainly God I was interested in talking to today. ☺ – with you guys playing and all . . .

Yeah, maybe I'll see you.

Stine

From: Stine Forsberg
Sent: April 06, 2003 8:46 pm
To: Mikael R. Andreasen
Subject: Re:

Today was good. Thanks.

Yeah, it was really, really good – to such an extent that I was ready to cry when I got home. I simply couldn't control my tears. Maybe because it was so beautiful, so tempting and so sad . . . etc., all at once.

From: Mikael R. Andreasen
Sent: April 06, 2003 9:07 pm
To: Stine Forsberg
Subject: Re:

I am really happy that you like coming to our church. Your enthusiasm is quite overwhelming. In retrospect, God is alluring, and if you think so too, then it's not that strange.

From: Stine Forsberg
Sent: April 06, 2003 9:22 pm
To: Mikael R. Andreasen
Subject: Re:

How can you think it's overwhelming that I want to go? Well, I guess I can partly understand it since only a short while ago I was too scared to even go. However, I thought my big bleak dream was clear. The desire to be allowed to feel that in some way that which seems to work so perfectly for you, is in reality right for me too. Yeah, the thought of God is alluring. I can't say God *is* alluring yet, because I haven't met him. ☺ Could be that I should invite him over sometime next week.

I think it's nice to go to your church. I was talking a bit with Sarah – since she had already thought about it – of going to that introduction-thing, together. I am a little curious and she has never been to it. She seemed to be interested.

– – –

From: Mikael R. Andreasen
Sent: April 06, 2003 9:39 pm
To: Stine Forsberg
Subject: Re:

Overwhelming simply because no matter how much I believe in God, it's still the exception when a non-Christian friend of mine wants to go to church. Also, maybe because it hasn't been that long since we began talking together about God and faith.

I think it's great how you, seemingly, get along so well with a lot of my friends. It's good that your impression of Christians is not only based on me. It would be cool if Sarah and you went to that introductions-course-thingy . . . if only because Sarah is so great to hang out with.

138

_ _ _

From: Stine Forsberg
Sent: April 06, 2003 9.56 pm
To: Mikael R. Andreasen
Subject: Re:

I completely understand your point. However, I want to make it clear that everything has changed since I met you. My thoughts, and also me. ☺ (OK, that probably sounded pretty dumb.)

You have introduced a lot of new things to me, even though I have of course thought more about them. There were also a lot of thoughts about God and faith in me long before we talked about it.

However, as I said before, done in a completely different manner and context. Not to mention a completely different viewpoint. To think back to a year ago, I would have been surprised at myself for having come this far in relation to God and faith. Even six months back I would have turned my nose up at the thought of it . . .

Now I'm glad that you think it's nice I get along well with your lovely friends. I'm glad that you don't feel it's presumptuous of me, or that I'm moving in on them. ☺

From: Stine Forsberg
Sent: April 28, 2003 0:33 am
To: Mikael R. Andreasen
Subject: Re:

My day has been good. So many things are happening at present. In my head and all around me. I really wanted to talk to you after the meeting today, but ended up talking to Flemming for almost forty minutes after you had left. It was great. He is so cool to talk to. It was touching because he said he had been keeping an eye on me over the past weeks and was glad that I had taken part in so many things, even communion. And happy that Mai had been praying for me. He said he especially had me in mind when he had asked everyone today to pray for those who hadn't yet met God. He said he felt that I really wanted to, and should.

I think the people that passed me on my way home must have mistaken the tears running down my cheeks for those mourning a boyfriend who had just walked out. ☺

Love,

Stine

From: Mikael R. Andreasen
Sent: April 28, 2003 1:08 am
To: Stine Forsberg
Subject: Re:

Mai told me briefly that she had prayed for you today. The conversation you had with Flemming sounds so interesting. I think it's great that this faith-process (wherever it ends up) involves believers other than just me – but I have already mentioned that before. I feel like I should write more to elaborate, but I can't find the words. In any case, it's fantastic that you apparently enjoy hanging out with these holy Christian girls. They are all amazing – and seem to think the same of you.

From: Stine Forsberg
Sent: April 28, 2003 3:39 pm
To: Mikael R. Andreasen
Subject: Re:

Yeah, it's great that I can tear myself away from you, so you don't stand accountable alone for all the big questions. ☺

From: Stine Forsberg
Sent: May 04, 2003 10:20 pm
To: Mikael R. Andreasen
Subject: Re:

I've had a strange day today. I appreciate the meetings so much since they open so many doors and give me insight into so much of myself that it's become an experience from another dimension. I feel so small, yet meaningful. I reach out with the knowledge that my happiness lies in the love I can give to other people. That in itself is inspiring beyond all imagination. It's unnerving, though, to put too much emphasis on one direct experience. Perhaps God is a gentleman, though, and isn't too pushy. Maybe he knows more than me and therefore awaits with his troops and lots of good things to come to invade my life. ☺

I speak to God a lot. I send him greetings all the time. The communication is unfortunately only one way. I probably only notice his presence through other people. Which in one way or another means that I can feel his presence. But not really, ultimately. It's complicated. And perhaps you don't understand. Sometimes I would love to be able to invite you into my head. It would undoubtedly make things easier at times. ☺ I do hope though – since that's impossible – that I make myself understood well enough.

– – –

From: Mikael R. Andreasen
Sent: May 04, 2003 10:40 pm
To: Stine Forsberg
Subject: Re:

Exciting things that you're writing. However, I'm too tired at the moment to properly digest it all. ☺

– – –

From: Mikael R. Andreasen
Sent: May 06, 2003 7:37 am
To: Stine Forsberg
Subject: Re:

If you feel like turning up on Sunday at the Pentecostal Church on Drejervej, then feel free. Our friend Bo will be speaking about silence and meditation. Meditation has often been a taboo subject in Christian circles, mainly due to its associations with Eastern mysticism. Apart from all that, it's simply about being able to, and daring to, be silent.

Ultimately Bo knows a lot more about it than I do. In any case, he is always a pleasure to listen to. He also enjoys doing things in new ways. We are going to help him out by playing some music that will pave the way for his teaching.

– – –

From: Stine Forsberg
Sent: May 06, 2003 2:33 pm
To: Mikael R. Andreasen
Subject: Re:

About Sunday, thanks, I would definitely like to come. I may have an appointment on Sunday in Jutland, but if so I'll just change it to another time. I had already thought of altering my appointment since Flemming told me he would be sharing on something this Sunday which he thought I could benefit from. So, if I am in Copenhagen I would love to accept the invitation to Drejervej.

I am meeting up with Ann Kristin in a bit. There was just one thing I wanted to write . . . well, I'll have to do that later.

All the best on this boring (weather-wise) May day.

Stine

– – –

From: Stine Forsberg
Sent: May 06, 2003 7:43 pm
To: Mikael R. Andreasen
Subject: Re:

Hey hey!

Ann Kristin and I have just eaten ice cream in the kitchen. And drunk beer. And listened to Rivulets. And talked about this and that. I should say hi from her. I told her I was about to sit down and write to you. We have already touched on a lot of the things I wanted to write today. As a consequence of a lot of time spent in thought on my part, I have to simply dump the whole thing on you too. ☺

Anyway. Hmm. I have never felt as good as this. Really. I'm always happy – because there's so much to be happy about. I am very pleased with the developments that have taken place in regards to faith and actions. Though at times I get gripped by an overwhelming sadness (perhaps too strong a word to use). And a hope – and at times a despondency comes into view.

When you yearn for something that isn't tangible. Something that inevitably you are the only one responsible for opening up. Maybe that's normal in the faith-process . . . that when you mirror yourself in an ideal you are also forced to admit your faults and short-comings? What do you think? Does that sound logical? I feel at times it has become a solo race, and that can be quite difficult. A few people I know are, under-standably, frightened by all the developments. Because they feel like it's been so powerful, and don't quite get it. And I do understand that. It's just sad to see some of them draw back and not dare to mention the subject. If you don't talk about it together, then you just end up drifting apart from each other. Luckily I know a lot of people who take it very well. Not too much understanding perhaps, but definitely respect and space. That I am very lucky for.

It's hard, though, when some of your family and friends look upon the whole thing as though something's wrong. Because it's not. It's the exact opposite.

Something completely different . . . this always re-volves around me, I feel. ☺ And I hope that I don't forget to ask. How are you by the way?

– – –

From: Mikael R. Andreasen
Sent: May 07, 2003 11:27 pm
To: Stine Forsberg
Subject: Re:

Hi there,

I will get around to answering your email, but I just have to find the time.

I have been painting today and being very practical.

Tomorrow I am off to Jutland, but yeah . . . when I find the time. ☺

Goodnight,

– mik –

– – –

From: Stine Forsberg
Sent: May 11, 2003 11:45 pm
To: Mikael R. Andreasen
Subject: Re:

Hey hey!

It was lovely to see you today.

Like before, it was a good day. It was really interesting to be at Drejervej. So completely inspiring. I am glad that you told me about the possibility of coming along. As soon as I have packed my suitcase for the colony, I will sit down and try to meditate.

Just for ten minutes.

It could be great.

With silence.

And focus.

All the best in the whole wide world,

Stine

– – –

From: Mikael R. Andreasen
Sent: May 14, 2003 4:05 pm
To: Stine Forsberg
Subject: Re:

Hi,

Welcome back from the colony. I'm sure it was good.☺ I have just put up a kitchen table. I should have been a carpenter. You asked how I was, hmm, I'm good. Although I think I'm a bit stressed. Work is quite hard at the moment – add to that all the practical things in the apartment. On top of that I am feeling hemmed in by a lot of people who want my attention (it's OK, but inevitably it means they detract from the things you really want to do, and I am forced not to have a thousand things on the go). Now I just want to clean up a bit in the kitchen, after having put the table up. Then in a couple of hours I have to play soccer.

It would be nice if you came to Drejervej again this Sunday to catch the last part of Bo's teaching.

All the best,

Mikael

– – –

From: Stine Forsberg
Sent: May 15, 2003 4:05 pm
To: Mikael R. Andreasen
Subject: Re:

I would really, really like to come on Sunday. Thanks!

Last Sunday was incredibly inspiring. I haven't been at home though, to practise at all. However, I would definitely like to. I had thought of sneaking down to the water in the afternoon at the colony and sitting and relaxing on the swimming jetty.

That would have been so wonderful. And the thought sounded quite romantic. ☺

But I ended up falling asleep, or reading.

Now I need a shower, and then some tea.

And then some music. Loud and long.

All the best,

Stine

– – –

From: Stine Forsberg
Sent: May 19, 2003 2:40 pm
To: Mikael R. Andreasen
Subject: Re:

Mikael, Mikael, at the next opportunity you should ask about your commission – which you most definitely have deserved. ☺

Yesterday was fantastic. I was running in circles afterwards. I can almost not remember how I got home, since everything was spinning in my head. ☺

The teaching was so intense. I don't want to find myself in anything less than the state I was in yesterday. Everything else just seemed a little trivial for a while. I hope all of this is just a small taste of what's to come for me. ☺

If in reality that fantastic overwhelming sensation that touched me inside and filled me completely to the brim was God, then I hope he wants to come again. It was so beautiful. Just the thought of it brings butterflies to my stomach.

Really, really.

Now I'm going home from work.

I hope you have had a good day.

May God's peace rain down over you. ☺

Love,

Stine

– – –

From: Mikael R. Andreasen
Sent: May 19, 2003 5:29 pm
To: Stine Forsberg
Subject: Re:

Hi Stine,

Thanks for your email. It was so overwhelming to read. It's hard not to just sit and smile. Yeah, how can I really reply. Hmm. I wonder if it wasn't God knocking on the door yesterday? It sounds like it could have been him. I also enjoyed the evening very much. I just lost myself completely in the music. Had to 'wake' myself up numerous times to keep playing tight. I think we succeeded, in one way or another, to express God's peace through the music and Bo's teaching.

I should, come to think of it, pass on greetings from Bo and wish you all good things from God. He had asked me to do that after I told him that you came yesterday.

All the best,

Mikael

p.s. The commission you can pass on to someone who needs it more than I do. ☺

– – –

From: Stine Forsberg
Sent: May 19, 2003 5:29 pm
To: Mikael R. Andreasen
Subject: Re:

I would love to give you the world for what you have done for me. You should know that. I'm sure you've noticed though, because at times I have difficulty in hiding my appreciation. I was thinking mainly that it was God's job to reward you. It is his company after all. ☺

Flemming always says he sees a 'red thread'. Well, he didn't to start off with. So as not to frighten me off with an inevitable, from my understanding, superior knowledge. However, now he won't let up. ☺

He is fun. I am soaked through, after recently having been subjected to the most crazy rain. But then I just imagined that it was God's peace raining down, as I had written to you earlier, and the experience took on a new perspective. ☺

If you happen to speak to Bo, please compliment him on his teaching which I thought was fantastic and totally relevant. He seems so sincere and good. I am very grateful that I have been allowed to become acquainted with his speaking abilities. Thanks for asking me if I wanted to come along.

All the best,

Stine

— — —

From: Stine Forsberg
Sent: May 21, 2003 0:30 am
To: Mikael R. Andreasen
Subject: Re:

Tra la la, today I have felt completely in love . . . all sorts of things are bubbling inside with excitement.

But I guess that I really am. In love that is. ☺

You can relax. It's with Jesus.

Stine

— — —

From: Mikael R. Andreasen
Sent: May 21, 2003 7:10 am
To: Stine Forsberg
Subject: Re:

That's completely amazing, your new love.

Congratulations, I think you'll make a great couple. ☺

Bye,

Mikael

EPILOGUE

I think there are several hidden points in the email dialogue that makes up this book, and I don't want to take away the joy from the reader in finding them. However, it's important for me to be allowed to comment on some of them. It's the whole reason why I, in the first place, chose to invite the reader to be part of this personal and private email 'conversation'.

The importance of giving people time and trying to meet them where they're at is probably the most important lesson I have learned from my written relationship with Stine. The importance of not – even with the best intentions – pushing people further than they are able to go.

And to just believe that God is in control, and does everything at his own pace. To *trust* that it isn't me who is saving this person – the *fact* that I can't is a completely different matter entirely. I can only endeavour to be available and open in relation to my faith. The most significant part of the process is up to God.

Sometimes I think we Christians, in our eagerness to lead people to Jesus, forget to actually listen to them: listen to where they are in their lives, listen to what they do or do not believe, or simply listen to whatever it is that they find the need to speak about. How important it is to approach people with a deep respect for whatever it is they might represent – and not an 'adopted' respect learnt in conjunction with 'friendship evangelism', but a *sincere* respect because we are standing in front of one of God's unique creations.

As Christians we are sometimes so focused on fruit, on harvesting the multitudes. So focused, I believe, that we sometimes forget the human responsibility that comes with bringing someone into the kingdom of God.

There is nothing so fantastic as people meeting God; I just think we need to become better at understanding people going through that process – that they have an extra need for someone to throw questions at, or vent their possible frustrations and doubts upon. That they know that there is someone who will listen. And it might end up requiring a large portion of your time, over a long period, but I think it's worth it. I asked Stine to formulate some of the deliberations she had during the time of our conversations. She wrote the following:

Before I met God, my impression of his overwhelming love was that it seemed clichéd, and
the thought seemed rather absurd. I have unfortunately, more times than I remember, been left
speechless and confused by the words that seem
to lose meaning every time they're proclaimed
by those people who feel they have the truth
inside them. My experience of Christians in the
past has unfortunately been mainly with those
who offer very little understanding, and have
little time to listen and offer support. It has been
'Jesus Loves You' and not much else, which I
consider a pity since, according to other Christians, those in evangelisation are serving the
highest calling. From my experience, the loud
proclamations I have stumbled upon have
always made the offer of salvation seem more
and more unattractive, rather than appealing.

I don't wish to put myself forward as the one who
knows the path – God knows I have made mistakes,
though of course he forgives. But after having had the
privilege of being a close observer of Stine's belief
process – yes, I do fear what would have happened if
I had simply smothered her with the gospel without a
lot of thought. If I hadn't taken the time to listen, and
given her the time to explain. Perhaps the essence of
the reality of this is captured in Søren Kirkegaard's
well-known words, which I chose as an epigraph to
this book. I at least *try* to adopt these words myself.

As I said before, there are a few things in the book that
I think are worthy of further thought. It is not my

intention to comment further on the problematic questions and theological depths which Stine and I have touched on briefly. Reflection and interpretation is handed over to you, freely.

In closing I would like to say a quick thanks to Stine for allowing me to publish this book. Also, I would like to thank my friends who in different ways have been a part of including Stine in their fantastic company. You know who you are.

'. . . also today there is reason to be thankful'.

Mikael R. Andreasen

NOTES

1 Together with some friends, I recoded an unconventional worship album that Stine happened to buy soon after she came to our little record store for the first time.

2 These are all names of bands that Stine would listen to.

3 On the internet music forum, where Stine and I first made contact, my signature is 'also today there is reason to be thankful'.

4 Taken from www.souljunk.com with permission from Glen Galaxy.

5 The downloaded mp3 is completely legal and freely accessible on www.mp3it.com.

6 Hanna's text:
My actions reflect a way of thought that is opposite

to my theoretical view of reality. I wish to save myself. I want to build a ladder up to God, jump up to his eye-level, wave my arms nervously – but continually – in the air and shout 'Look at me!'; force his arm up, so that he sees, and embraces, me. All accomplished by works; and in accordance with my deeply rooted understanding that nothing comes undeserved. In observance with this I make regular improvements: to pray more, read more, give more, do more. To live up to the biblical ideal! To be accepted by God. To be worthy of his fellowship. Almost as soon as the decisions are made, the reality sets in and exposes my powerlessness. Exhaustion and contempt for myself follow. For I realise – without a doubt – the impossibility of it. I cannot do it. Yet I want to. I wish to be as God desires, but I want to do it alone. Therefore I can never succeed.

In the attempt to reach God in our own strength lies the denial of my own condition, and the need for grace. The realisation of my inability leads to self-loathing. But thoughts carry on. God has set a standard that both he and I know it's impossible for me to reach. Despite that, he has set it. He knows my limits, but also his own power. His desire must be that I can reach the ideal, but not before I accept that it cannot be done without his help. Therefore I can rest in God. I will do anything, I acquiesce. Yet I admit also, that it isn't enough. He asks this, but not more. From then on it's God's responsibility. I can simply accept the help he offers. Then the motive for reading the Bible and praying becomes not trying to be seen by God, but seeing God. A desire to come closer to him, in the realisation that, I am already in him.

7 Svingninger is the name of the music forum where Stine and I met to discuss music. One day a new user appeared with the name of M. C. Kristen. He ended up adding nothing to the group and spent his time writing long sentences about the world's sinful and terrible state. Often his submissions were nothing but copied documents written by people like – for example – Moses Hansen [controversial Danish evangelist]. These documents had no other effect than to make people angry, and confirm their stereotypes of Christians. Sometimes people would attempt to enter into a dialogue with him, but he would just remain silent. For me, I saw the whole thing as an unsympathetic way in which to evangelise. He spent the whole time shouting at people, pointing out their sin and need for God, and yet when someone came with a question for him he didn't answer. Apologies from my side that there are such Christians out there.

8 Stine does not like New Year's Eve.

9 I received *Reaching for the Invisible God* by Philip Yancey for Christmas. I immediately lent it to Stine.

Prayer

Does it make any difference?

Philip Yancey

Multi-award winning spirituality writer Philip Yancey
is loved throughout the world for his honest, insightful
and inspirational writing. A journalist by training,
Prayer carries all the hallmarks of classic Yancey.
His quest to unravel the mysteries of prayer reads as the
journal of a fellow traveller: questioning, challenging,
lamenting the unexplainable and rejoicing in the
discovery of awesome insights. His journey is
beautifully illustrated with moving true stories drawn
from around the world.

Prayer tackles the following questions: What is prayer?
What difference does it make? Why and how should we
pray? What about unanswered prayer? How should
we understand prayer for physical healing?

Focusing on such a universal theme, this is potentially
Yancey's biggest book yet. To date, his books have sold
over 14 million copies, and have been translated into
25 languages.

ISBN 0340 909080

Hodder & Stoughton

www.madaboutbooks.co.uk
and
www.hodderbibles.co.uk